LOUISE WATSON studied Liter... Hertfordshire and spent several ... a Foreign Language abroad and i... Bournemouth, England and splits ... and writing. *Stop Making Your Life ... misery* is her first book and she is currently working on her second. When she isn't busy writing, she enjoys reading non-fiction books, practising yoga and playing the piano, although not all at once.

Stop Making Your Life a Misery

LOUISE WATSON

SilverWood

Published in 2014 by SilverWood Books

SilverWood Books Ltd
30 Queen Charlotte Street, Bristol, BS1 4HJ
www.silverwoodbooks.co.uk

Copyright © Louise Watson 2014

The right of Louise Watson to be identified as the author of this work
has been asserted by her in accordance with the
Copyright, Designs and Patents Act 1988.

All rights reserved. No part of this publication may be reproduced,
stored in a retrieval system, or transmitted in any form or by any means,
electronic, mechanical, photocopying, recording or otherwise,
without prior permission of the copyright holder.

ISBN 978-1-78132-236-9 (paperback)
ISBN 978-1-78132-237-6 (ebook)

British Library Cataloguing in Publication Data
A CIP catalogue record for this book is available from the British Library

Set in Adobe Garamond Pro by SilverWood Books
Printed on responsibly sourced paper

Contents

	Introduction	7
1	Wake Up	11
2	Stop Being So Nice	22
3	Stop Trying to be Something You're Not	34
4	Let Go in the Search for Love	44
5	Start Meditating	58
6	Start Doing Yoga	68
7	Stop Following the Flock, Follow Your Dream Instead	80
8	Start Trusting Life	91
9	Beware of the 'C' Word	100
10	Challenges of Going through 'The Change'	111
	Conclusion	121
	References	124

Introduction

When I look back on the first thirty years of my life, I feel exhausted just thinking about the amount of time I spent feeling worried or depressed, angry or frustrated. For someone who led a pretty ordinary (read: boring) life most of the time, the amount of mental drama I went through seems extraordinary.

I was never a happy person. Even as a child, I was the 'moody' one in my family and at school. I was always having a tantrum, crying and screaming about something. I was always anxious, always nervous, often depressed. I worried about being late for school, I worried about doing my homework right, I worried about what I was going to do after leaving school, I worried no-one would want to marry me. I remember looking to the future and just seeing black.

As I got older, the tantrums (mostly) stopped but the unhappiness remained. I always felt I wasn't good enough; nobody cared about me; my friends always let me down; no-one fancied me; I wasn't good at anything; I'd never be successful.

Of course, it wasn't all doom and gloom. There was the odd happy moment here and there; getting a good grade at school; being accepted into university; getting a job; my first date. Looking back, I think these things made me happy because a) they gave me reassurance that I wasn't a bad person and b) they brought me hope. Each time something good happened, I dared to believe things would get better and that I would eventually become a happy person for real; a permanently happy person.

Alas, it wasn't to be. Wherever I went, the same patterns would repeat themselves. I'd feel let down by my friends; the bloke I fancied wasn't interested; the job would turn out to be rubbish; the same feelings of low self-esteem would emerge again and again. Each time, I'd sink further into despair. Why couldn't I just be happy? Wouldn't it ever get any better?

In between these disappointing episodes there would be times when my external world actually seemed pretty good, when I appeared to have no reason not to be happy, so I told myself and others that I was. But there was still a feeling inside that something wasn't quite right. The best way I can describe it is as a feeling of dread, of something being missing, of feeling somehow disconnected from the world and the people in it. Although this feeling was always there, I can remember noticing it particularly at times when I knew I *should* have been happy; playing as a child, laughing at something silly as a student, backpacking round Australia and most recently, a couple of years ago when I was thinking about how much I liked my job and the place I was living in. In that instance, I remember thinking, *Everything's going well, so why do I still feel like this?*

I concluded then that it was just the way I was; that I would always feel like that and I'd just have to live with it. So imagine my surprise and elation when, at the age of around thirty-four, I was sitting in my living room doing nothing in particular and I suddenly realised that the feeling had gone!

The relief I felt was tremendous. I couldn't believe that after all those years it had finally disappeared. During the months that followed I would sometimes just sit in silence and enjoy not having that feeling. I was so excited, I actually thought I might explode. Although nowadays I've got used to it not being there, at times I still check in with myself and think how relieved I am that the cloud has finally lifted.

Upon reading Eckhart Tolle's *A New Earth,* I discovered that this feeling – the 'background unhappiness', as Tolle (2005) calls it – is something that affects many, many people; people whose lives may not seem all that bad on the surface, people who appear to have so much to be thankful for and yet they feel unhappy or depressed and aren't able to say why. It's something considered so normal to them that they may not even realise it's there.

Therefore it is my aim in this book to tell you how I finally broke free of the negativity that blighted so many years of my life. Why should you take any notice of me? I'm not a psychotherapist, celebrity or spiritual teacher. I can't tell you how to get the best job, more money, a big house or the perfect partner. As I write this, I'm thirty-five, single, have only a part-time, casual job, live in a rented flat (albeit a very nice one) which I'm paying for out of my savings. In the eyes of society, I'm a bit of a loser. But I would suggest that that's precisely *why* you should read this book; I have nothing society tells us we should have in order to be happy, and yet I am. I'm happier than I've ever been and keep getting happier.

Does that mean I walk around in a permanent state of bliss and cartwheel my way to the supermarket? No. Do I ever have an off day and lose the plot occasionally? Of course. My life isn't perfect; I still have my moments. But whereas before I was unhappy even when I was happy, now I'm happy even when I'm not. It's probably more accurate (although slightly more vomit-inducing) to say I'm now at peace. When I'm experiencing any negative emotion, I know that it will pass. I'm no longer desperate to change my present situation; I'm grateful for what I have but still excited about my future. I now enjoy my life and have the belief that good things will happen to me.

This book is an amalgam of all that I have learnt throughout the last five years of self-help book and article reading and talk and class attending. I've included several examples from my own experience to demonstrate how these ideas and practices have worked for me. What I hope to achieve is to explain as clearly as possible how these teachings have changed my life for the better and therefore how they can hopefully help you too.

The past couple of years have been something of a 'spiritual journey' for me, a term which still makes me cringe a little as I write it. I had never considered myself a spiritual person before and was often intensely irritated by anybody who saw themselves in that way. I know from experience how sceptical some people are about anything that could be deemed 'spiritual'. With that in mind, I have attempted to streamline my words on these matters to get to the bare essentials; to what I've needed to learn and understand to navigate the sometimes confusing world of self-awareness in order to make it work for me.

And I have to make it clear that this book is about what has worked for *me*. I'm not claiming to have all the answers or holding myself up to be some kind of self-help expert. However, when your life has seemed like a struggle for so long and you finally see that there is another way, it feels natural to try to help others by sharing your story.

At the very least, I hope some of the experiences I've shared here will help you feel less alone. I hope you will see a different way of looking at some of the issues that may have affected your life up until now and above all, I hope that by the end of the book you will see that there is a way out of the cycle of negativity that can seem to be eternally repeating itself, even if you don't want to follow my advice exactly. There is a way out. And if you haven't found it already, let this be the start.

1

Wake Up

One melodramatic friend who only rings me when she wants something? *Check.* One boss who I'm scared to say 'no' to? *Yes, she's here.* Always watching TV on my own? *Yes, I do believe I am.* An inexplicable and ultimately doomed attraction to someone completely and utterly wrong for me? *Got it.* Lots and lots of crying?

Yep, it's official. I've buggered it all up again.

It was 2008, the year I turned thirty. I was living in Sopot, Poland, where I was teaching English as a Foreign Language. This had been my fifth attempt to find happiness in another country. All previous ventures had resulted in more unhappiness and frustration as I encountered the same problems and people in various different guises, all conspiring with the universe to make my life a misery.

This time, however, it had seemed things would be different; my life in Poland had initially been great. I met nice people, I liked my job, I had a lovely flat and a good local salary, my own company folder and pen. What more could a girl ask for? I truly thought I could live there forever; or at least for a very long time.

And yet, just five months after my arrival, I was in despair. I couldn't believe that the same patterns that had plagued my entire life had repeated themselves yet again. The promising start to my experience made it seem all the more cruel. It was almost as if all my problems had knocked on my door and said, 'Hi! Sorry we're a bit late, traffic was terrible. Can we come in? Oh, go on! Let us!'

In the past, my response would have been to slam the door in their faces and get out as soon as my contract was up, find somewhere else to go and start all over again; this had been my strategy for the past six years. Now, it wasn't an option. Apart from being emotionally and mentally exhausted, I finally had to wake up to the fact that wherever I went in the world, my life would be the same.

Sound familiar?

Have you ever felt like this? Like wherever you go and whatever you do, you get things wrong? Do you always feel like you're trying to fix things that are wrong in your life, only to have the same problems repeat themselves again and again? And again?

For years I wondered what was going on; why was it that I could never find any loyal friends? I was so nice! Why did I always end up being put down and taken advantage of? Why couldn't I just find a decent boyfriend? Surely I couldn't be that ugly! Why did I always end up being alone? And how come I ended up working for lousy companies so often?

When we're not happy with our lives, the logical conclusion we come to is that we need to change something. You hate your boss? Find another job. Your partner's being a pain in the arse? Tell them to change their ways or kick them out and find someone new. Can't stand your rented flat any longer? Well, buy your own house, what are you renting for anyway? Life generally getting you down? Simple: move abroad. It doesn't matter where you go. Life in another country guarantees eternal happiness.

So you change job, and your new boss is even worse than your last one. Your new partner seemed great at first but now they've become just a variation of your old one. You struggle with paying the mortgage and the upkeep of your house. You realise living in a new country presents its own challenges and you miss all your family and friends. You know; the ones you wanted to get away from in the first place.

Whatever we do to change our circumstances for the better, it fails to bring us the happiness we crave. Or at least, we're not happy for very long. As in my Polish experience, sooner or later, the same old problems come out of the woodwork.

So what's the problem?

'It's you!'

Every so often, someone would very kindly tell me that I was to blame for everything that was wrong in my life and quite possibly everything in theirs as well. I was too miserable, not enthusiastic or lively enough, too quiet, too boring or too fussy. I needed to talk more, do more or be more cheerful. I should be grateful for what I had and stop moaning about my life.

So I tried. I tried being more talkative. I tried being more cheerful. I stopped standing up for myself when someone had upset me so that I wouldn't be seen to be making a fuss. I stopped asking for what I wanted and went along with what was expected.

But the result was always the same. Despite my best efforts to change, I still had the same labels attached to me, everywhere I went. The same problems would always occur. Obviously, I wasn't trying hard enough, so with each new job, each new destination and each new group of friends, I would try harder.

Each time I failed.

Every so often, I'd find I couldn't take it anymore. I'd have a complete meltdown and collapse into tears, sometimes for days at a time. I was sick of trying so hard and not having anything change for the better. Sometimes I'd find a friend to talk to about my woes, but as I got older, I'd try to do all my crying alone as I got the message that nobody liked depressed people. When with my friends, I had to keep it to myself or risk being rejected.

The most dramatic example of this was when, at the beginning of 2002, my father died. Initially, my friends were supportive; sending the usual flowers and cards, offering to help if I needed anything. At that early stage I was numb from shock, which gave me the false impression that I was doing OK, all things considered. Then after a few weeks, I fell apart. The pain was both emotional and physical. I could literally feel my body aching all over. I was constantly crying or on the verge of tears. I often felt angry or like I was going mad.

With few exceptions, the friends who had promised to be there for me didn't want to know. They couldn't understand why I got angry or upset sometimes; they couldn't understand why I wasn't always sure if I wanted to go out or why, once I *was* out, I sometimes needed to go home early. They didn't see why I might be feeling depressed. One person told me I was determined to be miserable.

Once again, I felt let down, but I didn't want to be left all alone. So I suppressed my emotions to avoid making anyone angry. I stopped talking about my grief altogether and pretended everything was fine. I no longer showed my anger to those people I felt had let me down. But inside it was still eating away at me. Eventually, I decided my only real hope of feeling better would be to get as far away from the situation as possible. Having just completed my TESOL Certificate, I had the perfect escape route.

And so began my six-year search for happiness in foreign lands. First stop was Japan, then Italy, then Australia, then back to Italy before eventually ending up in Poland. Every new country I went to, I tried hard to be different. I tried to be more talkative. I tried to be cheerful and positive. I didn't even tell people my dad had died unless they asked me about my parents, not wanting to seem like a misery.

And each time I was told I was too quiet, negative, and miserable. Everywhere I went, it seemed my old life would replicate itself in the new situation. Trying to change myself and trying to change my external circumstances hadn't worked, so what the hell was going on?

It is you, but not like that

Throughout our lives, we all suffer from our ups and downs, starting from birth. I've often heard how childhood is a magical time; how children are completely worry-free. That it's a time when we're encouraged to dream; when we believe that anything is possible; when we spend our days running and skipping through fields and our biggest problem in life is deciding which tree to climb.

Well, I beg to differ. For many people, childhood is a stressful time, even if we've been brought up by loving parents. We're all shaped by our upbringing in one way or another. Every family has its problems and each child will react differently to the same situation. Added to that is the fact that children have very little or no control over what happens to them; they're dependent on their parents, who are human beings with their own flaws which will inevitably affect the way they cope with parenthood. Parents will make mistakes; unpredictable events such as a divorce or bereavement will happen. No child can completely avoid suffering.

As children we adopt behaviours and strategies to cope with each situation, and we form beliefs based on our experiences.

Although these may seem appropriate to us at the time, the problem is that we often take these strategies and beliefs with us into adulthood. For example, if you learned early on that the best way to keep those around you happy was to hide your emotions, then you may have difficulty expressing how you feel as an adult. If you grew up feeling unlovable, then that's the image you'll have of yourself in your head, so your experience of life will confirm your belief, until you take charge and learn to see yourself as a lovable person.

In our attempts to resolve these issues, we are always subconsciously looking for new people, situations and experiences that will be similar to those that were the original source of our unhappiness and pain. When these new experiences happen, they provide the opportunity for the emotions and feelings to be released, and the chance to deal with the situation more effectively. However, until we understand this, we see each 'negative' person and situation as the cause of our unhappiness. We adopt the same strategies we did when we were younger, thus ensuring that we stay stuck where we are in our own misery.

Only now it seems all the more helpless; we experience more negative emotion, more distress, more feelings of 'I never get it right' or 'everything goes wrong for me' and that's what we continue to attract.

And on and on it goes. We repeat this cycle until it eventually gets too much, and we're forced to stop. We're forced to wake up. We're forced to stop looking on the outside, and start to look within.

But what about all these other people? Aren't they to blame?
I sometimes used to think that my life would be perfect if I could just live in the world all by myself. Other people made my life hell; they were hurtful, insensitive, selfish or just plain

annoying. They took advantage and always let me down (apart from the ones who didn't).

One of the hardest things for me to accept when I started to look within myself was that when we have negative feelings towards another person, we are reacting to something that lies within ourselves. For most of my life I had been focused on how unfairly I'd been treated by the people in my life, so it was tough for me for to hear for the first time that my problems did not lie with them but with me. I was projecting what I hated about myself onto the other person. How could this be? How could I be to blame when someone had hurt me?

It's important to understand that taking responsibility for your life isn't the same as taking the blame and in no way excuses the bad behaviour of others. If someone mistreats you, of course it's not acceptable and if you're in an abusive situation, you need to leave. You have no control over what another person does; what you *do* have control over is your reaction to that person and the way in which you allow yourself to be treated.

When someone annoys you or makes you angry, stop for a moment and consider what's really going on. What exactly is it that is pissing you off? Then, be honest; in what way could you be the same? Or do they remind you of someone unpleasant from your past?

Sometimes it's not too obvious, so we have to dig deep. For example, I used to be friends with someone who I ended up hating because I thought she was terribly narcissistic. I thought she was inconsiderate, that she was completely self-obsessed; she thought everyone was in love with her and she was in constant need of attention. *I'm not like her*, I thought, *I've always been a good friend to her, and she's never given me anything in return. What about me? And I never think anyone fancies me, even though I'm much better looking than her…*

It took a while for me to notice that I thought I was the perfect person in comparison to this girl. Because I'd always suffered from low self-esteem, I didn't immediately think it was possible that I could be displaying narcissistic traits myself, but I was.

There are times when a person may remind you of an upsetting situation from your past. Think about the last time someone upset you. How did you feel? Can you remember when you first felt like that? What is this new situation trying to help you resolve?

When I first began to learn about this concept, I found it all very interesting, and instantly set about analysing everybody around me in an attempt to understand why they were all such bastards.

Obviously, I hadn't quite got the hang of it yet.

Eventually though, I had to learn how it applied to my own life and behaviour. It was difficult for me to accept that I'd created the negative circumstances in my life and that I was responsible for the way others treated me. Life was so much simpler when everyone else was to blame for my problems.

However, once we accept responsibility for our lives, we can develop the necessary tools to relate to people and deal with situations more effectively. Hard as it may be, try to be grateful for the 'negative' people in your life. They're there to show you what you need to work on in order to move forward in life. When we allow ourselves to feel how we do and let the emotions go, when we learn to deal more effectively with the situations we repeatedly find ourselves in, then we can start to move beyond these patterns. Usually, there'll be more than a few patterns to work through, meaning that once we've resolved one pattern, another one to work on will be revealed. As time goes on, you will become better able to notice your reactions to situations and the possible reasons behind them, making the process easier.

After learning about the way in which I had subconsciously created my own circumstances, I finally understood why it was impossible to find a place to settle down in eternal happiness. I couldn't change my personality overnight just because I had decided to. I couldn't manipulate the external world to make me happy. Nor could I run away to another country to escape my problems, as I'd been doing for the past six years. It hadn't worked because all the time what I had really been running from was my own pain, my own dysfunction and my own destructive behaviour.

Crikey.

I looked back to when my search for happiness abroad had started; I was trying to escape from the pain of my dad's death and the hurtful reaction of my friends. Looking back, I understand now that this could have been a chance for me to release previous pain and emotion, to let go of my reliance on other people for a sense of self-worth, to finally let go of the need to get love from people who didn't care about me and just appreciate the people who did.

But I didn't. I stuffed the emotion down, then ran away to country after country, hoping that each new location would be the place where I would finally be happy. So everywhere I went, I met more opportunities to deal with my issues; another disappointing friend, another man who didn't want me; another boss I was scared of. More time on my own, bemoaning my sorry existence.

It was only when I stopped running, when I stopped trying to control the external world, accepted things as they were and looked within myself that things started to change for the better.

Instead of going home to England and then jetting off to another destination, this time I stayed put. My second year in

Poland was spent pretty much alone, having alienated the one friend I had whose presence my social life depended on. But the time on my own enabled me to gain a better understanding of why I acted the way I did and why I was always drawn to certain people and situations. With a better understanding of myself, I was able to start breaking the cycle of negative behaviour and finally begin to transform myself and my life from the inside. It's been a long road and I haven't reached the end yet. I probably never will, but at that point in Poland I'd taken the first step.

And with that, the external world began to change. I managed to find full-time teaching work in England after years of trying without success. I was able to settle down at last and find a decent place to live. I began to meet people who treated me respectfully.

But I'm so messed up!

So, you now know that you're responsible for your life and you've likely got a lot of work to do to turn things round. How do you feel? Depressed?

Yeah, I did a bit, too.

Taking responsibility for your life is tough; after a lifetime of blaming other people for the things that go wrong, it's not easy to accept that the reason your life isn't working out the way you want it to lies within you. Especially if you, like me, find you have a mountain of issues to work through. The prospect of dealing with it all may seem far too much to face. I remember thinking that it would be easier to just give up and carry on being miserable. But once you've got over the shock of having an imaginary giant finger pointing at your face, you'll begin to see that you have the power to change your life. You'll no longer be a victim. Things won't just happen to you, and you'll have a choice over how you deal with the circumstances you find yourself in.

The best thing to come out of my Polish experience was learning that there was a way to end the negative patterns that had followed me all my life, and that there was potentially a way to end the constant unhappiness. And not only that, but I had the power to make that change happen. Now I just had to figure out how to use it.

My first job was to learn how to assert myself and to stop being pushed around.

No more Miss Nice Guy.

2

Stop Being So Nice

Nice.

It's a simple enough word. It's just four letters long, but like many other four letter words, it has the potential to get us into a lot of trouble.

For years, I tried my best to be nice and like most people, I thought that was a good thing. I tried so hard to please others, which added to my confusion as to why my life never worked out the way I wanted, or why I didn't gain the respect of those around me.

However, after learning how I was responsible for my unhappiness; I began to understand that people treated me the way they did because I was just too nice. I was beyond nice; I was a pushover, a doormat, a people pleaser with no personality of my own. I sacrificed my own needs and happiness in an attempt to please other people and make them like me. As this had been my main problem at the time of my Polish wake-up call, I knew it is was the first thing I had to work on to break out of the negativity that had defined my life up until that point.

One of the problems with being a doormat is that it's easy to fool yourself into thinking that you're just easy-going or laid-back, so before I tell you what has helped me get out of my people pleasing ways, take a moment to ask yourself some the following questions to help you decide which category you fall into.

How good are you at saying 'no'?

One of the most obvious ways in which being a people pleaser manifests itself is that you find it very difficult to say 'no', even when you're being asked to do something unreasonable or inconvenient. It may be that you're always meeting the demands of your partner, friends, family members or boss and not thinking of yourself.

I remember once when I was in my late teens, a friend asked me if I wanted to go to the cinema with her and some others. I had no interest in the film they were going to see but said 'yes' because at that age staying in for the evening seemed like a fate worse than death. Then she told me that they didn't have a lift and asked if my mum could drive us; obviously that had been the only reason she'd asked me to go.

Did I tell her to get knotted and put the phone down? Of course not; I asked my mum, who agreed to drive us when she obviously didn't want to so that I could go and watch a film I didn't want to see with someone who clearly wouldn't have asked me if she'd been able to get there herself. Even at the time I could see the lunacy of the situation but didn't see what I could do about it; I was too afraid of making my friend angry to tell her how I felt. The fact that she'd pissed me right off didn't seem as important as keeping the peace.

More commonly though, I had this problem at work. To me, authority figures had to be obeyed, even if I thought they were being unreasonable. The fear of finding myself out of favour with someone who had the ability to fire me meant that I was constantly agreeing to cover lessons at a moment's notice or teach classes at the weekends. I lived in fear of the telephone ringing in case it was my boss asking me to work extra hours. Before answering, I'd think of a million excuses as to why I couldn't do it, only to crumble when it came to the crunch. Then I'd hate myself for being so spineless.

I spent a lot of time just feeling exhausted. I was always either at work or thinking about lessons, or thinking about how angry I was that I didn't have any free time. At times my diet would suffer as I grabbed something insufficient for lunch or skipped dinner because I was too tired to prepare something after finishing work at 9 or 10pm.

How good are *you* at saying 'no'? Do you find you put the needs of other people first? Are you always exhausted through trying to do too much for other people? If any of this rings true for you, you may have slipped into doormat territory.

Are you always a shoulder to cry on?

In the past, I was always being drawn to somewhat dramatic and needy people as well as those who were domineering and demanding. If someone had a problem, I was always keen to help and show them what a great friend I was. I felt like I was always taking care of other people and listening to their problems but none of them did the same for me.

I'd be only too happy to listen to my friends' tales of woe and offer them a sympathetic ear. I felt flattered that they'd chosen me to talk to. It never crossed my mind that they were only turning to me because they thought I was a sad loser with nothing better to do.

The problem was that after being emotionally exhausted by listening to their problems, I'd be disappointed when I didn't get the same help in return. I could never understand why the people I'd tried so hard to help were so quick to make their excuses when I needed someone to talk to.

When did you last get angry? (Are you sure?)

Another symptom of being a people pleaser is that you don't get angry, except that actually you do. In fact you may (like I did) feel angry pretty much all the time, but you just don't show it. When somebody does something that really pisses you off you may stay quiet to keep the peace while inside you're seething with a rage that will inevitably come out sooner or later – usually over something much smaller than the original offence.

I spent so much time sitting alone, going over and over in my mind what someone had done to me. I'd be angry at them for treating me badly, angry at myself for not saying anything about it and frustrated that I always attracted the same kind of people, despite being so nice.

There were times when the anger inside me would just bubble over and I'd explode at the person who'd upset me. They would usually explode back at me but louder or, even worse, start crying. Either way, I'd end up feeling guilty and I'd have to apologise, even if I didn't think I had been to blame. It would be a lesson learned; my needs and feelings don't matter.

Except that they do; and so do yours. In *Reinventing your Life,* Jeffrey Young and Janet Klosko (1993) tell us how anger, "is a signal that something is wrong…Ideally anger motivates us to be more assertive and correct the situation". If you have trouble expressing anger, you need to learn to do so constructively. It's better to calmly tell people when they've done something that has annoyed you as soon as they've done it, rather than letting it build up.

How easy do you find it to express your opinions?

I remember once being asked what kind of music I liked and not knowing what to say. It wasn't that I didn't know; I just didn't want the other person to make fun of my taste in music; I didn't want him to think I was a saddo, so I replied with a lame 'anything really', probably leading him to conclude that I was a really boring saddo instead.

Needing to be liked by others means it's difficult to express your likes and dislikes or it can cause you to change your opinion according to who you're talking to.

If telling someone about my taste in music was a problem, imagine what I was like with current affairs! Whenever the conversation turned to anything 'big' I had little to offer because I'd be afraid that people wouldn't like me if I disagreed with them.

For me, it got to the point where I was so used to just fitting in with what other people said or what they wanted to do that I completely lost track of who I was, what I enjoyed and what my opinion was. Even if I did know, I'd usually keep it to myself.

The problem with doing this is that not only do you lose your sense of self, but others have no real chance of getting to know you. Perhaps they will accept you if you agree with everything they say, but if it's only a false 'you', what's the point? You'll still be living in fear of the real you being discovered and rejected and any relationship you manage to form will be flawed.

How good are you at making decisions?

Decisions can be a real headache for the people pleaser. The fear of doing something 'wrong' might mean that you spend huge amounts of time seeking the advice of others over what to do. Perhaps you are reluctant to spend money on yourself until someone else gives you 'permission'. Or you may be so concerned about how your choices affect those around you that you neglect to do what's right for yourself.

Even the smallest decisions can be tough. How often do you hear yourself saying you 'don't mind' when a friend asks you what film you want to watch or what music you want to listen to? Whenever I did this I thought I was just being easy-going and that I really didn't mind; until the other person would pick a film I had no interest in or music I couldn't stand. Then I'd think, *Why didn't*

I just say what I wanted? When you never express any preference it can also be quite annoying for those around you as they are always the ones who have to make the decisions.

We may genuinely think we don't mind, but if we stop to think about it and we're really honest, there's normally a preference that we're reluctant to voice. Try saying it out loud. You might be surprised and get what you want; if not, at least you've made the first step in making yourself heard.

These are just a few ways in which being a people pleaser may manifest itself but if any of these situations sounds familiar to you, you may also find yourself asking this question:

How come all these other people get to do what they want?

One of the most frustrating things for me was that I'd see other people all around me doing whatever they wanted and getting away with it. *How come she gets away with not turning up for work?* I'd ask myself. *Why is he so popular when he's so rude to everybody? Why is it that she's respected for speaking her mind but I'm not allowed to?*

WHY? WHY? WHY??!

You get the idea.

Well, the answer was probably that these people respected themselves more than I did. What's more, they knew themselves; they knew what their opinions were and were unafraid to voice them. They knew what they liked and didn't care what others thought about it.

So my first task in breaking the cycle, and yours too if you have the same problem, is to learn about yourself and what you want. You have to learn to respect your own needs first. The following steps are what finally helped me:

Try to see yourself through the other person's eyes

If you feel you're being taken advantage of, there are two possible reasons for this: firstly, it may be that the other person truly doesn't see what they're doing. If you don't speak up when you're unhappy about doing something, it may not occur to them to think there's anything wrong. The second option is of course that they do know what they're doing but they really don't care. Unpleasant as this may be, it can again help to try and understand how you may look to another person.

I had this chance quite literally when I was friends with someone who was even nicer than me. She'd agree with everything people said, changing her opinion to suit who she was talking to. She was constantly putting herself down, which was exhausting for those of us who had to keep propping her up again with compliments. She'd apologise for talking too much, then for not talking enough. She'd lend people money and then complain that she didn't get it back, but she was too scared to ask for it. She was lovely, but she was draining. Sometimes I just wanted to shake her and shout, 'Get a backbone, woman!' Of course, I didn't do that. That wouldn't have been nice.

And of course, as we saw in chapter 1, my irritation with her most likely stemmed from the fact that she was like me. Through her, I was able to see that always trying to please other people is not really a very attractive quality. People don't want you to be 'nice'; they want you to be real. If you don't respect yourself, nobody else is going to.

Ask yourself where your doormat ways came from

Where did you learn that the best way to be was to put others first? Did you grow up in a family or environment where your needs weren't met or your feelings were disregarded? It could be that you learnt that the way to avoid getting into trouble was to do what others wanted you to do. As a result you now feel that putting yourself first or expressing your own opinion would result in being rejected or even punished for your actions.

The reason for asking where these patterns came from is not to place blame on your parents or whoever helped form this idea in your mind, but rather to begin to see that your current fears are based on a situation from the past and not on anything that is happening now.

As an adult, you're unlikely to be rejected for expressing what it is you really want, but if you are, you can cope with that. The world won't stop turning, as I discovered when I finally ended up friendless in Poland. It turned out to be one of the best things that could have happened to me, for I learned that being alone really was preferable to being friends with people who used and manipulated me. You can survive without friends who don't respect you.

Learn to say 'no' (it's actually not that hard)

Once, when I was talking to a counsellor about my doormat tendencies, she asked me, 'What would happen if you said 'no' to your boss?' 'I'd get the sack,' was my reply. 'What? Just like that?' she said.

Suddenly, the ridiculousness of my fears became clear to me. My boss was never going to fire me just for saying 'no' to working outside my normal teaching hours. She couldn't.

So I started to practise saying 'no'. At first I'd make excuses; I'd say I was busy or I was going away for the weekend but as time went on (and I ran out of excuses) I got more comfortable with just telling the truth; that I wanted to keep my free time just as it was: free. I wasn't fired and I didn't get into any trouble.

Now I have no problem saying 'no' to other people, I actually quite enjoy seeing the look of shock on the other person's face when I say it (evidently I still give off pushover vibes, causing people to think I'll agree to anything).

Sometimes it will be hard. For example, when you get a person who refuses to take 'no' for an answer and will ask you for the same favour in a number of different ways with a variety of guilt trips or incentives in the hope that you'll eventually cave in and say 'yes'. Hold your ground. You can calmly tell them that it doesn't matter what they say; your answer will be the same. They'll get the message that you're no doormat. Most probably, they'll respect you for saying 'no' (a lot of people have trouble with it!) and even if they *are* angry with you, it won't be forever. They'll get over it. And besides, it's better than being angry with yourself for agreeing to do something you don't want to do.

It may be helpful to think about why people keep asking you to do things. It's not just because they think you're a pushover; most probably, they know you're reliable, you'll do a good job, and you get things done. It had never occurred to me before that my boss was asking me to do extra work because I was a good teacher, and she trusted me to do what she'd asked me to do and do it well. I was also one of the few native speaker teachers she had at the time that she could depend on. She was never going to sack me because she needed teachers; she wanted me to stay.

Spend some time rediscovering what you want

As I mentioned earlier, the fear of being left out caused me to hide my interests and opinions to the point that I didn't even know what they were anymore. If you have that problem, it could be useful to deliberately spend some time alone rediscovering what you enjoy doing and what your interests are.

I used to go anywhere my friends invited me so that I'd fit in. Since learning to enjoy my own company more, I've discovered an interest in writing, doing yoga and trying to play the piano. I don't feel the need to be around people all the time, so if I don't want to go out dancing, I say so. I don't even give an excuse;

I just say I don't want to go. If that gets me labelled a miserable sod, so be it.

Being popular with other people isn't worth it if you have to spend your time doing things you don't enjoy. Besides, those around you can probably tell that you're not enjoying it, which won't help you in the popularity stakes either.

Examine your reasons for wanting to help others. And be honest!

If you find you're always giving to your friends and getting nothing in return, look at your reasons for wanting to help. As I mentioned earlier, I used to feel that my friends always came to me with their problems. I'd make them cups of tea and listen sympathetically while they sobbed about their latest boyfriend crisis, and I'd try to give them advice as best I could (which would normally go something like 'dump the tosser').

Then when I needed help, it was another matter. 'Oh yeah, sure,' they'd say, 'come round.' And when I got there a group of people would be there having a party. Or they'd just be too busy, or bring the subject round to their own problems again.

As I began to look at my own behaviour and reasons for helping others, I began to see that I had expectations behind my 'noble' deeds. I expected them to help me because I had helped them. I was helping them to prove that I was a good friend, in the hope of getting something in return. I wasn't giving from the kindness of my heart.

I used to have a friend who spoke to me all the time about her dramatic love life and how much emotional pain she was going through. Then she'd run off and have fun with all the people who were supposedly causing her so much pain and I'd be left exhausted, wondering why I'd bothered trying to help.

I began to think of her as an emotional leech, someone that I literally had to shake off so I could get on with having a life. Now

I have come to see that I was also a leech; sticking to her only to have a social life, because I didn't have much of a life of my own, because I didn't have any other friends and I was scared to be on my own even though I didn't particularly enjoy her company. I was using her as much as she was using me.

So be honest about why you feel the need to help people. Once you let go of any expectations of getting something in return, you worry less about being let down by friends. But having said that…

Don't worry about losing the friends who don't respect you

If someone is using you as a doormat, then you need to learn to assert yourself and stop being dependent on their approval. When you do that you're likely to find one of two things will happen; either they'll respect the new boundaries you've set and your friendship will grow stronger or they won't like the new you and the friendship will end. Let it; be thankful for the fact that they've taught you what you need to work on and move on to forming more positive, respectful friendships, which *will* come eventually.

At first, you'll probably find that you attract the same kind of person again and again, but as you feel better about yourself, you'll learn to walk away; knowing you can survive without any friends at all will make this easier, and eventually you'll begin to attract more of the kind of people you want in your life. When you decide what your boundaries are and let people know that you expect to be treated with respect, you'll find that your relationships with others will begin to improve.

I've found that I no longer attract friends who try to take advantage. Occasionally, I meet the odd person who tries to boss me around, but I see it as a good opportunity to practise being the new, more assertive me. And I haven't had a demanding boss for years.

It can be hard to break the habit of trying to please others; the pattern has been developed over a lifetime and won't disappear overnight. Learning to assert yourself involves becoming more comfortable with the thought that someone might be angry with you or (gasp!) not like you. I know in the beginning I still failed to state my needs at times and got angry with myself for 'failing'. Then I'd go beyond assertiveness and fall into aggressiveness instead and get angry with myself for getting angry. As Young and Klosko (1993) remind us, it's important not to do this but rather to celebrate any progress you've made.

Even when you learn to assert yourself more, the uncomfortable feelings don't always go away, either. Just before I left my last teaching job I had a pang of guilt when I said 'no' to covering a lesson for my boss when she'd said she was 'desperate'. But I was also pleased that I'd put myself first; I knew she'd find someone to do the lesson, and any annoyance she might have felt towards me would pass.

Be brave, take control of your life, learn to say 'no' and stop worrying whether people like you. Be honest about what you like and dislike. Dare to give your opinion, even if it's 'I have no opinion.' With each step you take, you'll begin to feel better about yourself. When you stop being so nice to others and start being nice to yourself first, you'll find that those around you will respect you more. Those who don't will simply fall out of your life and if that means everybody, it will only be temporary. For that time, at least you'll like the person you're alone with.

Only when you're true to yourself, can you begin to grow and start leading the life you were meant to lead.

So stop trying to please everyone, or I'll be really upset with you.

3

Stop Trying to be Something You're Not

When I look back on my life, I can hear a multitude of comments in the voices of various friends, colleagues, teachers, bosses and complete strangers, all with one word in common: 'quiet'. I heard it all the time:

'You're very quiet, Louise.'

'You're so quiet!'

'You're too quiet. Why aren't you talking?'

'What?! You went out last night? But you're really quiet!'

As you may have gathered, I'm a quiet person. I work on a need to speak basis. I'm a shy person but I'm also an introvert. And yes, there is a difference. As a shy person, I get nervous when talking to people I don't know and as an introvert I still don't always feel like talking, even when I do feel comfortable around someone. I don't feel the need to be around people all the time, and I'm bored rigid by small talk. It would seem that in the eyes of many, this is a deeply flawed way to be.

Being told on an almost daily basis that I was too quiet until I was about thirty led me to think there was something seriously wrong with me. I'd cry into my pillow at night, wishing I could be more outgoing. If only God would make me louder all my problems would be over.

However, over the years I've come to realise that it's not just shy people and introverts who have trouble. Extroverts get told they're too loud, emotional people are told to get a grip, but those who don't show emotion are cold and unfeeling. If you're a calm person you need to liven up, if you're lively you need to calm down. If you're a bit different you're weird but if you like a simple life you're boring.

It seems you're never going to please everybody, regardless of your personality. So my aim in this chapter is not to whine about how tough it is being shy or introverted, although I'll be doing plenty of that too. What I want to address here is the importance of accepting yourself fully as you are, regardless of what other people think of you.

The need for acceptance

It's human nature to want to feel accepted by others and we learn from an early age that in order to achieve that, we need to conform. As children, we need to be good to please our parents. When we go to school our teachers get to tell us how to behave. In the playground, we learn that we need to fit in to be part of a group of friends. The loneliness of being left out is hard to take, as is the feeling of displeasing those who have authority over us. So we do (or try to do) anything to ensure that we are accepted.

Perhaps, to fit in with the cool group, you'll pretend you don't like reading or you don't really want to join the school choir, but although hiding your true interests is detrimental to your well-being, it is easy to do in comparison to changing your entire personality at the flick of a switch.

I always felt, deep down, that it was wrong for anyone to tell me I had to change; that apart from being rude, it was pointless. Every time someone told me I should speak more I felt like saying, 'Oh, speaking! Now, why didn't I think of that?!' I got so much criticism for being quiet that obviously, if it had been as simple as just speaking, I'd have done it.

My friends, I thought, should just accept me as I was. Strangers should, quite simply, bugger off and talk to someone else if I was boring them, but there was one group of people that I thought must have a point: authority figures.

Authority knows best

I normally did well at school; my work would get good comments and grades, I stayed out of trouble and didn't upset anyone. Schoolwork was just about the only thing I thought I was good at, so I'd look forward to report day when I could read about how marvellous my teachers thought I was. The positive comments were usually there, but more often than not they were accompanied by something like 'Louise is very quiet in class; she should really try to speak up more.'

I'd feel really frustrated every time I read these remarks and more than a bit confused; with the exception of French and Spanish, it was only my written work that was being assessed, so why did it matter if I didn't speak up in class?

When I started work, the comments continued. In one appraisal, my boss gave me glowing feedback about my work and attitude, praising me for just getting on with my work without complaint. But there was just one weakness he wanted to talk to me about, which was that I was a 'bit quiet'. He might as well have just said, 'Well, your work's great but there's just one problem. Now, what was it? Oh, yes, that's it; *your personality.*'

Again, I didn't think it was fair. My job was data entry; I didn't need to speak. What he meant was that *he* didn't like my quietness. As it didn't affect my job, he had no right to call it a weakness.

That was what I *really* thought, but I'd still come back to the same answer: *My teachers think it's important that I speak, so it must be. My boss sees a problem with me being quiet, so there has to be a problem. I must be wrong. They must be right, because they're in charge. They know best.*

As children, we're led to believe that our parents and teachers know everything. The majority of us accept what they say without question. Unfortunately, this submissive attitude often follows us into adulthood; even if we don't like them, we believe (subconsciously at least) that our bosses are in authority because they're better people and therefore when they tell us what's wrong with us, we'd better get down to fixing it as soon as possible before we get told off, fired or face some other life threatening calamity.

Well, I'm here to tell you that it's all rubbish.

Your bosses, teachers and (with respect) your parents are just people with an opinion.

Just because someone has a certain job title, wears a suit and has an allocated parking space, it doesn't mean they have a right to put a label on you. If your parents say something negative about you, the fact that they're older and they raised you doesn't make it true. I've yet to experience parenthood, but I have been a teacher and for a brief period, I was a (very low level) boss. Both experiences led me to understand that people in authority are no different from those working for them. Your teacher, parent or boss is a human being with their own fears, insecurities and hang ups. The only difference is that their position or role in your life allows them to take their insecurities out on you and dress it up as feedback or guidance.

Being a teacher with several different personalities in my class gave me an insight into what it was like to be 'in charge' of people who didn't always 'fit in' with my way; who (dare I say it?) I didn't always like. I'm afraid I wasn't always as accepting of others as I would have liked to be.

Did I want to put a gag on the student who wouldn't stop talking? Sometimes. Did I get annoyed when I'd spent, ooh, minutes planning an activity and the shy student refused to take part? Yes, I'm afraid I did. Did I feel like walking out when the opinionated student told me I should be teaching grammar and that my lessons were boring? Hell, yes. I'm sorry to say I didn't always hide my annoyance, but after learning not to blame the students for my irritation I began to be curious about my feelings. Why did these people upset me so much?

The talkative student was threatening my sense of control; if they didn't belt up, who knew where my lesson might end up? We might not even get on to the reading activity! Oh, the shame! The shy student threatened to send my lesson down the toilet by refusing to speak and reminded me of my own inability to keep a conversation going. The opinionated student just scared me; with them in my class I felt incompetent, and I lost any feeling of authority I had over the class. But these people were simply being who they were, just as I was being who I was. They couldn't magically change their personalities any more than I could and who was I to say they should?

Another reason why authority figures feel the need to criticise occurred to me when I had to write reports for the quiet students I taught. I was always reluctant to write that word, knowing the effect it had on me when I was at school. I tried to focus on how good they were at writing or grammar instead. However, there were times when a student hadn't produced any written work at all, meaning the only thing I knew about them was that they were quiet. So I'd have to write it in their report: *Takashi (made up student) is very quiet and should try to offer more answers in class.* I'd hate myself for writing it, but when I did, something dawned on me.

*

They probably didn't give a shit

My teachers and bosses probably didn't care that I was quiet. They had to write something for me to work on so they wrote that; my work was good, so that's all they had left to say. What's more, my teachers at school had about twenty-seven reports to write for each class they took; they just wanted to get them all done and watch *Fifteen-to-One*.

I can just see my old teachers now: 'Louise Watson? Which one's she? Oh yes, the quiet one. Rightio; *Louise should speak up more in class. Next…*'

I'm not saying all teachers are lax (although a lot of mine were), but school reports can be hard to write, especially when you've got loads to do and you're trying to think of something original to say on each one. So if you're still haunted by the words of your old school teachers, remember that they probably didn't really care what your personality was like, and even if they did, their opinion doesn't matter unless you agree that it's a problem.

The error in corporate cloning

Managers are also told to give their staff something to work on. Unfortunately, there's still a belief in the world of work that we need to work on our weaknesses to become good at everything. I've only recently come to understand the error in this way of thinking after reading John Williams' *Screw Work Lets Play* in which he states that it's far more productive to focus on what we do well rather than worrying about our weaknesses (2010). We're human. As humans we're going to be different from one another, and as a result we're going to be better at some things than we are at others. To think otherwise is completely unrealistic.

I've never come across any shy person who suddenly became a brilliant public speaker because they were forced to speak when they didn't want to. I've never witnessed anyone miraculously becoming an admin wiz because they've been berated by their manager a million times. When you're always trying to improve on your 'weaknesses', your work can only suffer as you're constantly fretting over what you're not naturally good at, rather than getting on with what you do well and producing the best work possible in that area.

One of the reasons I decided I needed to work for myself was because I could no longer tolerate the corporate insistence on creating an army of robots with identical personalities to form their workforce. It seems to me that companies are intent on stamping out any form of individuality to match some arbitrary definition of what a good employee should be. This approach is not only unrealistic but demoralising for employees.

It's also pointless; just as I would always have the 'quiet' comments, my colleagues would tell me that they too had the same remarks about *their* personalities given to them over the course of ten or twenty years. Why didn't they just change to stop the comments? Because they *couldn't*; it was the way they were. Telling others to be different from who they are achieves nothing but upset for the people in question. So some advice for you if you're ever thinking of doing it: don't.

Why fitting in is bad for you

It's hard not to be affected by other people's opinions, even when you understand logically that their opinion means nothing. When you're always being told to change, it's hard not to believe there's any truth to it and the natural conclusion to come to is that you have to do what it takes to try to fit in.

Throughout most of my life I tried so hard to change. Every time I went out with friends as a teenager and young adult, I'd get roaring drunk so that I'd talk more and be more fun. Every time I started a new job, I tried my best to think of more things to say, to join in with conversations. I read self-help books and searched the internet on how to overcome shyness. But nothing worked; it was never enough.

Still the 'quiet' comments came. Most frustrating of all was when I thought I got on well with someone and then they'd comment on how quiet I was. I didn't understand what else I could do, so in the end, I just gave up trying.

I'd like to say this decision came as part of some profound realisation that I was beautiful and perfectly imperfect and the universe loved me the way I was, but the truth was, I just couldn't be arsed. I was fed up with putting my energy into trying to change for other people and not succeeding, especially as actually, I didn't particularly think I needed to change; I knew being shy wasn't helpful to me but I also knew I was worth getting to know and felt I should be accepted as I was.

I was shy. I'd just have to deal with it. I'd already done a lot of things in my life that my more outgoing friends were too afraid to do. As long as my shyness didn't stop me doing the things I wanted, I could live with it. If I wanted to talk, I'd talk. If not, I didn't. Everyone else could swivel.

Then, weirdly, I found the comments pretty much stopped. The few remarks on my quietness I still received were made only as a passing observation, sometimes even as a compliment. The last time I was told I was 'too quiet' was over a year ago (by my boss – of course!) and I can't even remember when the last time before that was.

After that last comment, I had a look at myself. Am I quiet just because I don't feel like talking or am I afraid to speak? I came to realise that it's a bit of both, depending on the situation. I feel awkward around new people but I sometimes just don't want to talk. It was then that I began to understand the difference between shyness and introversion. My shyness makes life more difficult. That's something I need to overcome. My introversion is another matter. It's just the way I am and I wouldn't be able to change it even if I wanted to. It may make others uncomfortable, but that's not my problem.

I now see that in trying too hard to change, especially when I didn't really want to, I was denying who I really was, which exacerbated the problem. I felt nervous around others, and then so did they around me. When I stopped trying, and just accepted myself the way I was, I became more comfortable with myself, and as a result attracted more people willing to accept me as I am.

As Brené Brown writes in *Daring Greatly* (2012), 'Fitting in is about assessing a situation and becoming who we need to be in order to be accepted'. When we try too hard to fit in, we suppress the person we truly are, so that we end up feeling isolated and alone anyway. If you decide to change, make sure it's because *you* want to, and not because somebody else thinks you should.

Again, remember that if you do decide you need to change, it will happen gradually. There are times when I still get nervous and I'm tempted to start telling myself how useless I am, but I have to remind myself about how far I've come. Years ago, I was so chronically shy that I wouldn't leave the house on my own. The only exception was to go to school. I was scared of getting a bus on my own, scared to talk to people in shops, scared of speaking on the phone, and speaking in public? Forget it.

Since then I've travelled to the other side of the world on my own and I've spent the last eleven years teaching for a living. My students were surprised when I told them I was shy, they thought I was so witty and confident (yes, really). It's not that my shyness doesn't make life more difficult sometimes, but as long as it doesn't stop me achieving what I want to do, I'm happy. So when you're tempted to be harsh on yourself, just think about how far you've come and give yourself a big pat on the back for your progress.

If you want to find acceptance among others, the key is to like and accept yourself first, fully as you are. This doesn't mean that change won't come if that's what you want, but it means the change will come from within. Once you've accepted all of you instead of fighting against your supposed flaws, then the pressure is off, and you're likely to find you'll change naturally as your confidence grows. Then you'll find you draw more of the right people into your life.

4

Let Go in the Search for Love

Do you have a friend who is always single? You tell them they can bring a guest to your party but you know they'll come alone. In your single periods, you're comforted by the fact that they'll always be there until you find someone new. Perhaps you have a colleague with a question mark over their head. You know; the one who lives alone and is the only one never to bitch about their exes. You assume it's because they've never had a relationship but you're too polite to ask. Or maybe it's someone in your family; an aunt or uncle who always seems to be alone. Occasionally you might whisper amongst yourselves, 'What's the deal with him/her? They're not *that* rough. Are they just not interested? What's going on?'

Or maybe that person is you. Crap, isn't it? Well, at least you're in good company; I'm that person too. At thirty-five, my love life has consisted of a few disastrous flings which could never be described as 'proper' relationships. I've spent years wondering what's wrong with me, crying to my friends, clinging to any man that showed any interest, before pretending to accept that I was meant to be alone, which lasted until I met the next man for me to obsess over.

With such a disappointing record, it's hard for me to write about love. I've spent much of my life on the outside looking in, believing it was something that happened to other people and not to me. But I'm going to do it now for all the long-term singletons out there.

Why most dating advice doesn't help

Over the years, I've read numerous books and articles and watched several programmes to help me understand where I might be going wrong. I've found few helpful; most work on the assumption that you've had several past relationships, or that you have a multitude of would-be suitors to practise their tips on. Most annoying of all are the books that tell you how to keep your current partner happy. *(Erm, I haven't got one; that's why I'm reading your book!)*

Very, very rarely do they address the possibility that their reader may not have a lot of experience, or that they never go on dates and that they don't even know how to go about getting one. But it happens. There are people of all ages who have found themselves, for one reason or another, in the 'professional singles' club; people who have been single all their lives or for so long that they don't see any way that things could possibly be different.

The fact that this has so seldom been addressed added to my despondency about being alone, and I'm sure it has had the same effect on others. It gets to the point where you feel ashamed to admit to your lack of a romantic life. You think you must be the only one; that you're a freak and that love really is something that is not meant to be in your life.

'It'll happen when you least expect it'

Oh yes, my single brothers and sisters, I know you've all heard that one. The implication of this statement is of course that we need to stop worrying about not having a partner, live life to the full, enjoy ourselves in Single Ville and then hey presto, Mr. or Miss Right will magically appear. I can see the logic in that argument; we're more likely to be attractive to another person if we're happy and not desperate for a partner, but it's hard to be positive when we're always being reminded that we're on our own by some of the comments we get on a regular basis:

'Why aren't you married? You're beautiful!' (*Well, it must be because I'm a bitch, then.*)

'Aw, you'll meet someone.' (*Thanks, but I've only come in here to enquire about a mortgage.*)

'When I met Bob I wasn't looking.' (*Really? That must've been your secret twin sister who told me she was on a mission to get a man.*)

'You need to love yourself first.' (*Well, stop reminding me that nobody loves me and I might stand a chance.*)

'You should get out more.' (*This is the first time we've met. And we're out.*)

Even the 'positive' comments from others have added to my fears and feelings of isolation. As I've got older, I've noticed that there's an assumption that I've made a choice not to get married. Being told, 'You've done the right thing staying single' makes me feel that it's now a permanent part of my life that can't be changed.

I know all these people mean well, which is why I've resisted the urge to stab them with a plastic fork, but comments like this are unhelpful to a single person and will only make them feel worse. Constant questions about why I'm single only lead me to ask myself, *God, what is wrong with me?* They also imply that life without a relationship isn't worth living, making it all the more difficult to love life like we're always being told to if we want to attract a partner.

So to sum up: we're supposed to love ourselves before anyone can love us but nobody has ever loved us so we feel unlovable and therefore unable to love ourselves. Then we're supposed to be happy before we find a partner so we try to be happy in the hope that we'll find a partner to make us happy and then we find we can't be happy because we're always being reminded that we're single and unhappy.

Confused? Yes, I was.

Well, I think I've finally worked it out, for after years and years of trying, I've found myself in a place that for so long seemed both impossible and contradictory; I can now look forward to meeting someone and yet not have my happiness depend on it.

So how did I get here after so many years of feeling sorry for myself?

Know that you're not the only one

As I said, the loneliness of always being single can be exacerbated by the feeling that you're the only one in that situation and therefore there must be something wrong with you. Now I don't have statistics to back this up, probably due to the fact that nobody wants to publicly admit to their lack of experience, but I've seen enough evidence on internet forums and problems pages to know that professional singlehood is not *that* uncommon.

In some of my more self-pitying moments, I've gone looking on the internet for other people of my age in the same situation and have found people in their twenties, thirties, forties and older who have never even been on a date. This can happen for a variety of reasons; lack of self-esteem, social anxiety, trust issues to name but a few. What saddens me is the amount of people I see who just accept that now it's never going to happen. I went through a similar phase in my late twenties, but luckily it didn't last long, and just think about how sad it would be to believe it's all over at such a young age. I'm thirty-five now; I could have another fifty-odd years ahead of me. Can it really be too late? Only if I believe that's the case.

But what if I *do* die single and childless? Surely it's better to die having lived a life of fun and expectancy rather than doom and gloom because I haven't met 'the one'. Or even one.

We have to get out of this negative thinking pattern; not so that we'll attract a partner but so that our lives can be fun regardless of whether we do or not. So let's move on to some of the common beliefs that get us down when looking for love.

Stop telling yourself: 'I'm too old, skinny, fat, ugly, boring…'
(insert other negative adjective of your choice)

I've never had a lot of confidence, but as I got into my late teens, I began to realise that I wasn't ugly, I wasn't thick, I had a good sense of humour and I was generally a good person. Sometimes I thought I was too shy; maybe *that* was why I didn't have a boyfriend! Well, maybe not. Being shy doesn't help, but assuming this is the only reason I'm single would ignore the fact that there are plenty of shy people who are married or have partners.

In *Calling in the One* (one of only two books on relationships that I've found useful) Katherine Woodward Thomas (2004) writes, "What you have is a reflection of what you believe you can have, and your relationships are a prefect mirror of your relationship to yourself". If we don't like the person we are, physically or otherwise, that will only be reflected back to us, which then only serves to confirm our beliefs. If I tell myself I'm too shy or quiet to attract the man of my dreams, then the result will be that either I stay on my own or I'm only going to attract men that tell me I'm too shy and quiet, thus reinforcing my low self-esteem.

It takes time to learn to accept yourself after years of feeling that there's something wrong with you, but a good place to start is to look at the reality of the situation; how likely is it really that your supposed flaw is preventing you from having a relationship? Think you're too fat? Look around at all the fat people in the world with partners. Think you're too ugly? Is everybody you know in a relationship *really* drop-dead gorgeous? I don't know what you look like or what kind of personality you've got, but I can tell you this; whatever the answer, that's not why you're single. Come on! Even serial killers get married! There must be hope for us. There has to be another reason, which leads me to my next point, and you might not like it…

Ask yourself: Do you really want a relationship? No, I mean, *really*?
OK, I know I'm venturing dangerously into annoying git zone here. I've had personal experience of fighting the urge the punch somebody in the face when they've told me that I was the one holding the possibility of a relationship at bay.

One such occasion was during a drunken conversation I had in a hostel in Perth, Australia. My drinking partner and I were the last ones up one night, finishing off a carton of particularly cheap and nasty wine and chatting about our disastrous love lives. I'd just told her about a man I'd been besotted with years earlier who'd left me heartbroken, the rat. She told me that I didn't really allow people to get close to me. I thought it was the most ridiculous thing I'd ever heard. After all, wasn't I being open by sharing my story with her? And I *was* ready for a relationship with the man I'd been talking about, he just didn't want me! How dare she suggest that I didn't want to be with someone? How utterly insensitive of her!

It wasn't until about three years later that I finally saw it. After having learned about how we repeat certain patterns in relationships, I wrote down the names of all the significant people in my life with a brief outline of what had happened in each case. When I had finished, it was suddenly staring me in the face; I only went for men who were unavailable to me in some way. They would either be attached, on the rebound, not able to choose between me and someone else or just not interested in a relationship. Often, they'd show me enough interest to make me think something would happen and then pull back or keep me dangling and clinging to the hope that they might change their mind. Which of course they didn't.

However, when someone *was* actually interested in me, I always found something wrong with them; they were weird, they were too keen, their nose was too big, they stared at me too much, they were rubbish kissers, they were too nice, they were too geeky.

Seeing this on paper made me realise that my hostel friend had been right; I was completely sabotaging any prospect of finding love. I wanted a relationship, but I didn't *want* a relationship.

Weird.

Not only that, but each rejection I received reinforced my belief that I wasn't lovable. What I began to realise is that we humans are all basically bonkers; we stick to what we know, even if it's unpleasant. I didn't want to be alone, but it was all I knew. I always thought I wanted a loving relationship but when it looked like it might happen, it freaked me out because it wasn't something I was used to.

So look for your pattern. If you've always been single, look back at the people you've been interested in. What do they all have in common? Once you've identified what your pattern is, you realise that you can do something about it. You're no longer just randomly getting yourself in a pickle with one unsuitable (potential) partner after another. You see that you have a choice, which takes me to my next step.

If you see an old pattern emerging, have the courage to walk away

I don't know how many times I've clung to the possibility of a relationship with someone it was obviously never going to happen with, because I couldn't believe that I had done it again and I thought that this time, it had to be different, only to discover that yes, I had and no, it didn't.

It's obviously going to be tough to walk away from someone you're attracted to, especially if you've been alone for a long time. And you may well be single for a while when you decide to break your pattern, because it takes time to do so. You're likely to find that for a while you'll still keep meeting the same kind of people, in the same way you will when trying to change the kind of friends you make. As Woodward Thomas (2004) says, "It's as though the universe is testing us…Are you willing to stand in the void rather than compromise yourself again?"

So, you're still feeling attracted to the wrong people, and you know you should do the sensible thing and walk away but there's no-one else on the horizon. You might be tempted to think that having *something* is better than nothing, even if it's not good for you. Besides, being sensible can, quite frankly, get a bit boring. Sometimes, the thought of a little drama with Mr. or Miss Wrong may seem preferable to another night in on your own in front of the television.

But the time alone will be worth it. It may take a while, but eventually you'll begin to feel better about yourself as you break the destructive cycle and stop believing the negative thoughts that may have dominated your life up until now. This, in turn, will lead to you attracting more positive people into your life, whether they're potential partners or just friends. Having people in your life who treat you well will then help to reinforce the new positive image you have of yourself.

*

Decide what you want from a relationship

It was only relatively recently that I even considered the possibility of thinking about what I want in a relationship; I'd always thought I would just be lucky to have one. What kind of attitude is that? No wonder people took advantage. Whenever I met someone I liked or started seeing someone, my thoughts were always centred round what they thought of me and whether I'd said or done something to put them off. I just wanted them to like me. It never occurred to me that I should be thinking about whether *they* were right for *me*.

But over the past couple of years, I've learned about the importance of thinking about all the qualities that you want in a partner. What do you want from a relationship? Don't know? In that case, think about the kind of behaviour in others that has disappointed you in the past and how you would like to be treated instead. If you've always been single, you can still look back on relationships with family members, friends or colleagues. Or look at the relationships you've witnessed that you wouldn't want to be in; what would you like in a relationship that is different from theirs?

This approach to defining what you want has the added bonus that you may even learn to be grateful for the negative things that have happened to you, as they've caused you to want something better for yourself. I've also found myself being grateful for all the time I've spent alone; looking at all the bad relationships I've witnessed has helped me to decide what I want for myself and be willing to wait for it; I don't need to be scared of being on my own because I always have been.

Ask yourself if the kind of person you want would date you

I've already said your personality isn't why you're single and it's true; anyone can get *someone* if they really try hard enough.

However, as has been stated by several writers and teachers on this subject, if you want to attract the kind of person you want, you need to be that way yourself. In other words, don't look to that person to make up for what you perceive to be your shortcomings.

I used to think I wanted somebody confident and happy so they could pull me out of the rut that I was in. I also wanted someone really good-looking so that I'd be reassured that I wasn't unattractive. *If only I had a nice boyfriend I wouldn't have to spend all my time in front of the TV.* I actually thought like that. *Life would be better if I had a boyfriend. If I had someone sexy and confident like Derek (made up name)* then I'd feel better about myself.

But why would the sexy, confident Derek want to waste time trying to drag me away from the television and put the effort into making *me* feel sexy and confident when he could very easily find someone who was already like that?

I still don't have a nice boyfriend, or even a horrible one. I also don't have time to watch TV. I have no idea how I found the time to sit in front of the box just a couple of years ago. Now when I'm asked about my free time and hopes for future I have something to say for myself and I can see that I'm a much more attractive prospect for someone than I used to be. I can believe the sort of person I want would want me too because I'm closer to being that kind of person myself.

Stop saying, 'But I want that person!'

One of the biggest obstacles to finding happiness in Single Ville is unrequited love. This could happen because they're an ex who broke it off with you, or it might be, as is often the case with a long term singleton, that nothing has happened between you at all. You just fancy them and haven't had the nerve to do anything about it. It could be that they're nothing more than a passing acquaintance, and yet you can't seem to get them off your mind.

We've all done it (erm…*haven't* we?). We meet someone nice, think they're hotter than a hot thing, they appear to be everything we're looking for; good-looking, kind, caring and funny. They seem to be the perfect package. Then we discover that they love Marmite too and suddenly we're convinced the search is over.

Infatuations like this can be alluring for several reasons. Firstly, unless you just go for it and ask them out, you don't know for certain that the feeling isn't mutual, so you can continue to make up little scenarios in your mind about how you'll get together and fantasise about waltzing up the aisle and decorating your living room. Secondly, as you don't really know them, you only see their positive side, meaning you can fill in any blanks yourself and turn them into anything you want them to be. Finally, the insanity of the situation can lead to the assertion that it's 'meant to be'. 'I don't even know him and yet I can't stop thinking about him!' you cry. 'Surely, that must mean we have some mystical connection and we're meant to be together forever!'

Maybe.

But probably not.

Perhaps these obsessions don't really do any harm. After all, as long as we keep it to ourselves and don't become stalkers we can just be happy until we finally meet someone who wants us. But if they go on for too long, they can start to get a bit weird; perhaps you spend too much time looking at their Facebook page, or you analyse everything they say and do: *Ooh, he said 'Hello' to me today. I wonder what he meant?* Even if you never tell the person in question, you feel like you're going mad because the situation makes no sense.

When I was in this situation a couple of years ago, I was genuinely baffled by my obsession; I knew the person wasn't interested, I even knew that we were so different that I probably wouldn't be happy with him anyway and I also felt I was already happy in my life; I didn't feel lonely at the time. I didn't think that I was desperate for a relationship.

So what was going on?

I searched for answers in several books, talks and internet articles and discovered that when we're focusing our attention too much on another person, it's a sure sign that we need to look within ourselves. There's likely to be something missing from our lives, even though we may not even realise it; there's a hole that we're convinced can only be filled by another person. But however wonderful the other person may be, they're not *that* great. I remember, years ago, crying over someone who didn't want me and I suddenly thought: *This is mad. A year ago, I didn't even know of his existence. I managed all right without him. Why am I feeling like this?* What I didn't realise then was that the answer didn't lie with him, but with me.

Think about what it is that attracts you to them. Are you sure you're not trying to make up for some perceived flaw of your own? For example, if you don't see yourself as attractive, perhaps you feel being with someone really good-looking would boost your self-esteem. Or if they're particularly intelligent or profound, then maybe you want them to save you from your life and look after you in a way that you feel has been missing up until now.

If you're looking for another person to fill some perceived void or deficiency in your life, you can be sure that it isn't really the person that you want. I was stunned by how quickly my last obsession diminished after hearing this. It disappeared pretty much overnight when I realised that his attractiveness and friendliness were something I was hoping would fill a void in my life.

It can also help to look for other ways to spend your time. I realised that I had too much time on my hands; too much time to think. When I filled my time with more creative pastimes, when I was engrossed in writing or learning to play the piano, I had no room in my mind for thinking about my imaginary boyfriend.

What we need to understand is that it's not the person we want, but the feeling that we think they're going to bring us. We think we will feel better with them in our lives. We see them as the source of our happiness, not realising that the source of our happiness is within us.

When you know that, you can work on feeling that way without a partner. If you want to feel more loved, then try giving love to others; be a loving person. Then you're more likely to attract the type of person you want, because you are that way yourself.

Stop saying, "But I want a partner now!"

There will be times when you find yourself wondering, *I've done the work, where's my partner?* Despite my new positive attitude, there are times when I have to admit that I get impatient. It's like I'm waiting for my reward to come for working so hard on myself and I'm saying, *Come on universe! Isn't it about time you send me Mr. Perfect? What more do you want from me?* This tells me that I still have work to do. I tell myself this feeling will not last forever, it will pass. I felt excited and happy before and I will again. My impatience is just my old pattern returning to try and make me miserable.

Although I'm still single, I've noticed that recently more men have shown interest in me. More men have asked for my number and I've been asked out more often than before. While I'll admit that's not exactly difficult, this increased interest shows that *something* is happening. I haven't grown a new face, so something must be changing on the inside that has made me appear more attractive on the outside.

We need to relax and enjoy doing the work on ourselves that we want and need to do. When you can learn to do that, it's possible to fully expect to meet someone but to let go of the neediness and the yearning. Learn to enjoy the journey, and you will be happier.

5

Start Meditating

Up until my early thirties, I thought meditation was something done by only two groups of people: *deeply profound and spiritual people and pretentious arseholes who thought they were deeply profound and spiritual people.*

I, of course, fell in to neither category. I had no idea what these people were talking about and could not understand how sitting cross-legged with your eyes closed for hours on end could possibly help change your life for the better.

Nowadays, however, meditation is an essential part of my daily routine, so either I was wrong for all those years or I've now become a member of group two. I like to think it's the former, but I'll leave that for you to decide as I explain why I'd now recommend everyone start a meditation practice. Later on in the chapter I'll also be outlining some of the possible problems you may face along the way. But first, the positives.

I think, therefore I am. A neurotic mess, that is.

Most people would agree that it's impossible to stop thinking; we're all pretty much of the opinion that we must always be thinking about something, and often that something is pretty negative: *I'm too ugly. How the hell am I going to pay the bills? Why does everything go wrong for me? I can't believe the bitch said that! Who does she think she is?*

Conversations generally revolve round complaining; about the weather, our jobs and bosses, not having enough money or about what so-and-so has done. It's considered normal. So normal that we don't realise it's a problem.

For me, a large proportion of my thoughts used to revolve around worrying, with each negative thought leading me down a road towards more and more stress, fear and despair. Say I'd make a mistake while teaching; I'd go home and fret about it all evening. I'd be imagining the students complaining to the school, after which I'd be hauled into my boss's office to be interrogated and probably fired; then I wouldn't be able to get another job because they wouldn't give me a reference. *Then* what would I do? I'd never work again. Before I knew it, in my mind I'd be destitute and living under a bridge somewhere (not sure why moving back to my mum's wasn't an option when I was in Worry Land).

As you've probably guessed, none of these fears came true. Nor did most of the other things I've worried about over the course of thirty-odd years. And on the few occasions that they did come true, it was never as bad as I'd imagined. But no matter how many times I told myself this, I just couldn't stop the thoughts going round and round my head.

But there is a way out. Through having a daily meditation practice we can learn to observe our thoughts, slow down our minds and better understand what's going on when we have a negative or fearful thought. Perhaps we can't always control what thoughts come into our minds, but we can learn to take less notice. And when we do that, the mind begins to quieten down. It's almost like it's noticed you aren't listening and gives up. We no longer need to be overcome with negative thoughts and worry about what might happen. We can then take this practice into our daily lives and begin to use the mind to create our best selves rather than allowing it take over and run havoc with our lives.

The benefits that meditation has so far brought to my life are as follows:

Reduced levels of negative thinking and worrying! Yippee!

While worry is created by thinking about the future and what might happen, meditation trains us to focus on what is going on *now*. What's more, we begin to notice when our mind has wondered (as it always does) and once we've done that, we can bring our attention back to the present. In time, we can cease paying attention to the negative thoughts that come in.

I noticed how much better I am at not worrying when I left my last job after nearly a year of procrastinating. When I told my colleagues I was going, I was met with the following questions:

'Why?' (Answer: *because I don't want to teach anymore.*)

'Are you just really unhappy?' (*Well, no, not really.*)

'What are you going to do?' (*I don't know; I'd like to try writing.*)

'What kind of writing?' (*I don't know.*)

On the surface, my choice made absolutely no sense whatsoever; I was leaving a job that I wasn't unhappy doing to do something I knew very little about and which might not earn me any money for ages, if ever. I should have been terrified but although the negative thoughts came creeping in, they failed to take hold.

Years ago, in the same situation, I would have been a wreck within a week of leaving work; worrying about making money; telling myself I'd messed things up and made a terrible mistake. The opinions and questions of others would have added to my conviction that I was an idiot. Now, although those thoughts still come in from time to time, they stay in the background. They attempt to drag me down, but fail. Over time, I've come to see my mind almost like another little being inside my head which is trying to lead me back into my previous life of misery. Only now, I no longer allow it. When I find myself drifting into worry about the future, or I see that I'm starting to beat myself up over the choices I've made, I'm able to stop myself before going too far and bring myself back to whatever I'm doing right now.

Increased levels of calmness.

As you progress through your meditation practice, you'll notice that you become less bothered by the long queue in the supermarket or that colleague who's always stealing your stapler (although I still struggle with controlling my anger at technology that refuses to work properly, no matter how many times I shout at it. I'm not perfect, you know). The little things that used to make you want to scream will no longer ignite such rage. In fact, a long queue can become the perfect chance to practise.

It's not that the negative thoughts and feelings don't arise, but when you meditate regularly, they are allowed to just be there and then pass, whereas without meditation you may be tempted to hold on to those thoughts, repeat them again and again in your mind, share them with others, and make them bigger and bigger until your negative emotions consume you, affecting not only yourself but those around you.

A calmer approach to life will bring benefits to your relationships with others. You'll be able to notice when anger or irritation arises and learn to choose your reaction, rather than exploding with anger or snapping at someone automatically.

Higher levels of concentration

Less mind clutter helps to improve your focus, whatever your task may be. You're less likely to be distracted by others or stressed out by the clock ticking away. In fact, you might even start to feel like the clock's ticking more slowly.

Once I'd been meditating for a while, I began to notice an increase in my ability to concentrate on one task alone. I'd be busy preparing my lessons in the school staffroom, and having got through quite a chunk of work I'd be convinced it must be time to go to class. But then I'd look at the clock, and think, *What? It's still only 8:50?* I'd be stunned to see how little time had passed and how much I'd managed to get done in just a few minutes. It seems strange that the more time you spend apparently doing nothing, the more time you seem to have to do the things you need to get done, but it's true.

Increased levels of creativity.

Meditation creates more space in which the ideas can come through (Alidina, 2010); it makes sense that when you're not consumed by thinking pointless or destructive thoughts there's more room for ideas to come to you. Freedom from negative thinking will also help you take your ideas and explore their possibilities without rubbishing them with thoughts like *Ah, that'll never work* or *I wouldn't be able to do that.*

I was always good at writing, but my previous attempts to pursue it as part of my career were pretty half-hearted and died a premature death as I struggled to think of ideas. Whenever I sat down and *tried* to think of something to write about, nothing happened. Since starting a meditation practice, the ideas just come flooding in, especially when I'm not trying. This can happen during meditation but sometimes I can be simply lying in bed or doing the washing up and an idea will come. The moment I start trying too hard to think of something interesting or witty to write, the ideas dry up.

These are just some of the benefits that I have experienced; there are many more reported physical and mental benefits besides the ones I've outlined here. However, to be able to experience any of these you need to practise regularly, and at the beginning this can be tough. Some of the difficulties I faced when I first started meditating were:

Feeling stupid

In early 2012 I went on a mindfulness weekend retreat, during which the rest of the group and I were required to do a walking meditation which entailed walking slowly around the dining room table, paying attention to each and every step and what was going on in the body. As my mindful companions and I were walking at snail's pace around the dining room table, I was cringing inside. I thought it was the weirdest thing in the world. All I could think about was what my friends and family would think if they could see me. I tried to tell myself that they couldn't. That everyone in the room was doing the same thing as me. But it was no good. I felt stupid; I was embarrassed.

Later, my mindful host asked us to give our thoughts on some of the practices we'd done throughout the weekend. I was honest; I said I didn't see the point of the walking meditation and was worried about what I looked like.

My host told me that when you start taking control of your mind, it doesn't like it. It says, *'ere, hang on a minute. I've been in charge all this time and we've got along perfectly well. I'm the boss and don't you forget it.*

When you start to take control of your life, the mind will try anything it can to convince you that you're making a big mistake. So the thoughts come in: *Oh, come on! You're wasting your time! What would your friends/family/colleagues think about this? You can't even do it properly, look – you're still thinking!*

There have been times when I've even felt embarrassed while I've been meditating on my own! But the words of my mindful host always come back to me; I know the embarrassment and negative thoughts are my mind trying to take back control. As I've persevered and continued with my practice, the thoughts and feelings have faded.

Too much thinking

For someone who can quite happily sit and do nothing for hours on end, it was (and sometimes still is) remarkably difficult for me to meditate. A common recommended technique is to count the number of breaths as they go in and out of the body. When I first tried, it usually went something like this:

> 1, 2, 3, 4…I can't believe he said that to me, who does he think he is? No, I shouldn't think that, I'm too spiritual now, he didn't mean to be such a turd…oh shit, I'm supposed to be meditating…1, 2…bloody hell, shell suits were awful…

I tried, I tried again, but I couldn't stop the thoughts coming in. I got very frustrated. Like many people, I thought the purpose of meditation was to empty the mind of thoughts and if I couldn't do that, I'd failed.

In one meditation class I attended, the teacher explained how the mind usually goes into one of three areas; remembering the past, planning for the future or imagining things that haven't happened (yet). It's the nature of the mind. The purpose of meditation is not about emptying your mind of any thoughts at all. Through meditation, we learn to *observe* the mind; the thoughts may still come but we can let them pass without paying as much attention to them as we once did.

So each time you find that your mind is wandering, simply

bring your focus back to the breath and start again. The fact that you've noticed is a good sign. It means…you are meditating!

You don't have time

Then you *really* need to meditate. Make time. Start with just five minutes a day; or even one if that's all you can manage to begin with. Make it part of your daily routine, picking a particular time and sticking to it. Slowing down will help you to think more clearly and your increased ability to focus will help you work more effectively, which will eventually lead to you saving time.

You worry about doing it right

Over the last year or so I've attended classes, read books, and watched copious YouTube videos on the subject of meditation. Each time I was searching for a simple answer to one question; how do I meditate properly?

However, with every class and every video, it seemed like I was just sitting there with my eyes closed. What was the difference? How did I know if I was meditating for real?

One of the problems for me was that there was so much conflicting information.

The one constant instruction was to sit up straight. Even that was difficult for me as I had possibly the world's poorest posture. Then we're told that we *should* be cross-legged, but if you can 'only' kneel or sit in a chair that's fine (so which is it?). Then for how long should we meditate? Some say fifteen minutes, others say about half an hour, but I've also heard you should meditate a minute for each year of your life. Then what should you do with your eyes? I always thought you should close your eyes, and that's what happened in my classes. Then I read that you should have your eyes open and looking at an image or another point of focus. Then I heard they should be open half way and you should look at the end of your nose.

It seemed that every time I tried to learn more about doing it right, I heard something else that contradicted what I'd learned before.

Very confusing.

Finally, I decided the only real hope I had was to go to see some *real* meditators. Yes, that's right; Buddhists.

I live very close to a Buddhist Centre, but fear had always stopped me going to their meditation sessions whenever I'd toyed with the idea before, although I'm not quite sure what I imagined they were going to do to me. However, after so many months of wondering if I was really meditating, I wanted to know for sure. Surely the Buddhists would tell me.

It looked promising enough as I entered the shrine room. We were given some information on getting in the right position and then the session leader read us some passages from a book about meditation. So far, so good. Then we were told to sit with our eyes half closed and try not to move. Unfortunately, I'd chosen the wrong position to sit in and my little legs were already getting achy after a couple of minutes. I still found it hard not to drift off into thought and couldn't get comfortable. At one point I was finding it so hard to focus that I decided to have a look round and see what everyone else was doing.

I came eyeball to eyeball with the session leader, who'd obviously had the same idea as me.

I'm not quite sure what I was expecting, but I was rather disappointed. *Great*, I thought, *even the Buddhists can't show me how to meditate*. I wanted to know exactly what to do. I wanted to be told, 'Yes, that's right; you're well on the way to enlightenment. Well done.' Oh well, at least I'd got a cup of tea and a slice of cake out of it, something that had been missing from the other classes I'd been to.

Afterwards, I reflected on my expectations. Maybe there was no real 'correct' way to meditate. Maybe there are just different ways and you need to find which one's right for you.

So I stopped stressing over doing it 'right' and just got on with it. I'd do a little every morning, watching the breath, gradually increasing the time I spent practising. When I was *really* struggling to focus I found guided meditations useful in helping to stop my mind from wandering off so much. When I stopped worrying about doing it right and I began to settle into a daily practice that worked for me I started, in time, to notice the benefits.

Meditation can be difficult at first and takes perseverance. Even now I still feel resistance sometimes when I sit down for my morning practice. But stick with it! When you learn to deal with the thoughts or discomfort that occur while practising, you can then take that with you and apply it to the challenges you face in the 'real world'.

What's that? I sound like a pretentious arsehole? Well, don't take my word for it. Try it for yourself and see.

6

Start Doing Yoga

Initially, my goals upon attending a regular yoga class were as follows:

> To become less stressed out and anxious.
> To improve my posture and thus get rid of my backache.
> To avoid anyone who had an Om tattooed on their back
> (or anywhere else).
> To refuse to do any chanting whatsoever.

As you might have gathered, I was slightly dubious about this yoga thing; I was still slightly traumatised by the fact that I was now meditating and I was afraid of going too far down the road of pretentiousness. However, my hosts on the mindfulness weekend were highly enthusiastic about the benefits of a regular yoga practice, and they seemed all right. One of them had been the epitome of everything I wished to be; calm, laid-back and unpretentious. Maybe I could give it a go and I could become just like him.

Besides, I wanted something to do in my free time that wasn't too strenuous. In that sense yoga ticked all the boxes; a non-competitive exercise class where I can move really slowly and have a nice lie down at the end? Count me in!

My plan was simple: turn up; go to the back; do as the teacher says; leave.

I had no idea about the effect that yoga would have on my life, but it hasn't all been rosy. As I am now a born-again positive person, let's start with the pluses:

Physical benefits

There are numerous reported physical benefits of doing yoga, many of which I'm still learning about as I continue to practise. As well as helping me with the ailments I knew I wanted to get rid of, it has also cured me of some issues I hadn't even realised were there.

Before attending yoga classes, I suffered from constant back pain. I can't remember when it started but it had been there for so long that I just accepted it as part of my life. I knew this was probably due to my poor posture. My shoulders were hunched over, and I had a weird 'S' shaped figure; although I was a UK size 6, I didn't have the flat belly I was often accused of having. When I looked at myself in the mirror sideways, I actually looked like I had a pot belly, only the lower back went in, creating a kind of 'S' with my body; far from attractive. Usually I just consoled myself by looking at the front of my body, which still looked good.

Gradually, as the weeks and months passed, I began to notice a decrease in the pain, until it had gone completely. Then one day, I was shocked when I happened to look in the mirror and – what was that!? A normal looking lower spine! A flat belly that didn't look like a fat belly! Result!

The effect on the outside of the body is only part of the story, however; I hadn't realised the effect my lousy posture would have on the internal organs. But it now makes perfect sense; when a person is hunched over, their organs are pushed together, so it shouldn't be surprising that they can't work as well as they should. As my chest began to open up, I noticed an almost frightening increase in the amount of air that was now filling my lungs as I breathed in. It felt like my chest was going to explode; obviously I hadn't been using my lungs to their full potential!

After about six months of practising, I also noticed I just couldn't eat certain foods anymore; junk food was out, and ready meals were an absolute no-no. After a while, I couldn't have the daily packet of crisps I used to have with my lunch, and perhaps most shockingly of all, it became a struggle to finish a glass of wine. Just what was happening to me?

I've found this happens to many people who start practising yoga regularly; they find that they naturally become more conscious of what they eat and generally start to look after themselves more. As a result, I know that I feel healthier, more energetic and I've been told that I look well, whereas before I was always told that I looked tired.

Mental and emotional effects

Poor posture and squashed up internal organs don't just affect us physically but emotionally as well. When your body's not working to its full capacity and you're all bent over you're unable to feel good about yourself. I just thought I'd spent too long hovering over a computer at work, but now I see that my hunched shoulders were likely an attempt to hide myself. In turn, my body suffered inside and out, which added to my lack of self-worth.

Now my body was opening up, all my internal organs were getting back to full working order and increasingly, I found that I started feeling better about myself. Certain thoughts and feelings occurred to me that hadn't been there before. In particular, I began to question things that were going on at work. I became increasingly aware that I was capable of doing more. I was now able to speak in front of a lot of people; wouldn't it be good to use that to do something bigger? To help people on a larger scale? I could write well; maybe I could write that book after all. Maybe I could write articles or a blog. Perhaps I could finally try my hand at acting.

Suddenly, after years of thinking I had reached my full potential by becoming a teacher, I began to realise that I was capable of doing much, much more; that I hadn't even scraped the tip of iceberg.

Slowly, but surely, I began to make a realisation: I would have to leave my job.

Sorry? What? I asked myself again and again. *Come on, Louise, this is the job in England you wanted for years! You know, the one that was going to bring you security? The one which would finally help you to settle after years of running from yourself? Won't you be running away if you leave now? What are you thinking, woman?*

It seemed ridiculous. Nonsensical even. Especially as I didn't dislike my job; I didn't love it as much as I used to but there were still lots of enjoyable aspects to it. So why did I have to leave? For a long time I was in turmoil; I was afraid to leave the security I'd found in my life after so long, especially as I didn't know what I wanted to do. But for me there was no going back, as much as I sometimes wanted to. It was almost like I had no choice. I just knew that there was something else for me to do and I needed to let go of the security of my job to find out what it was. I had to leave.

I was scared but thankfully my increased sense of self-belief was joined by increased levels of concentration and attention, higher levels of self-acceptance and an overall trust that I'd be taken care of no matter what happened. All of which helped me to retain my sanity as I ventured into the unknown when

I eventually left my job to finish writing this book several months later.

After a year and a half of practising yoga, I'm hooked and I can honestly say I'd recommend it to anyone. Yoga's ace. But I wouldn't be able to sleep at night if I didn't give you the full story, because as much as I love yoga, there was a period of a few months when I hated it at the same time. There's a darker side that few people (or in my case, no people) tell you about before you start.

To be honest, though, the first negative wasn't entirely unexpected:

Yoga can be bloody annoying at times

One of the scariest things about becoming immersed in Yoga Land was not discovering that my preconceptions about it were wrong, but discovering that they were right; yoga classes are full of really annoying people.

It's not just me that thinks so, you know. Do a quick search of the internet and you'll come across a plethora of articles and blog posts about how annoying yoga can be. Upon reading these, I recognised a number of characters I'd come across during my classes. For example, there was the heavy breathing student who made me feel like I was taking part in one massive dirty phone call. He also did his own thing in class to show how fantastically bendy he was, the bastard. Then there were the students who try to turn themselves into their teachers, banging on about 'energy' and how 'beautiful' everything is and despite being British, saying it all in an American accent. Why?

Then there were the teachers themselves; floating around being all spiritual and profound, finishing twenty minutes late because they're far too enlightened to worry about time. Some of the instructions were incomprehensible and all the talk about genitals and anuses was just embarrassing. And then there's the chanting, and the Oming. I mean, was it *really* necessary?

Gradually, though, something strange started to happen; I found that I started to like a good old 'Om' at the beginning of class (but I still hate chanting with a passion and am very grateful that my current teacher does none); I found myself resting in Child's Pose just that little bit longer to take my time, I began taking my watch off so I'd no longer get angry with the teachers who finished late. *Hey!* I'd tell myself, *Time only exists in our minds!* Although in reality the fact that I was getting twenty minutes of free yoga hadn't escaped me.

More recently, I found myself feeling a little smug at holding Crow Pose for longer than any of my classmates and informing a yoga teacher of five years that 'shanti' actually meant peace and not happiness (it could mean both for all I know, but it allowed me feel superior at the time). More and more, I found myself doing things I never thought I'd do; refusing alcohol, snubbing the staff party to go to yoga class, saying the word 'beautiful' in my head when I saw someone do a good Downward Dog (although I swear I've *never* said it out loud. And I thought it in a British accent).

Oh my God! I thought, *I'm turning into one of them; the yogis.* I struggled with this for quite a while. *Am I turning into a complete arsehead?* I asked myself. I could see myself becoming one of those people I'd always made fun of. I didn't want to go down that route, but I didn't want to stop practising yoga either. Whatever should I do?

As it happened the answer came when, after about eight months of attending classes, I found a new class much closer to my home with a teacher who was just a normal person who happened to do yoga. All my classmates were normal too; not a whiff of pretentiousness. And I was disappointed; I had nothing to moan about, nobody to make fun of. I found myself missing all the airy fairy talk I'd dismissed for so long. I longed for something deeper and more profound.

I'm glad to say I stuck with the class and have (hopefully) now been able to incorporate yoga into my life without turning into a clone of one of my teachers, but the whole experience got me thinking; why did those things embarrass me? Why did I get so angry with the people I met in class who probably hadn't even noticed I was there?

As much as I was tempted to write about how irritating everyone in yoga is and how perfect I am, we unfortunately can't dismiss the point made in the first chapter; that what we react to in another also exists in ourselves. There is a reason why these people annoy us so much; and we need to look within ourselves to find out what it is.

For example, the heavy breathing and free-styling student brought out my insecurities about being new to yoga. I wanted to be as good as him and show off to the class about how good I was. Instead I was hiding so people didn't see how bad I was, which was kind of arrogant in itself because it assumed everyone was interested in what I was doing.

If, like I did, you find yourself feeling smug or superior to others because of what you can do or the changes you're making to your life, be pleased. The fact that you've noticed is a good sign; you've realised you've attempted to adopt an identity of yourself as the 'spiritual' one and the very fact that you've noticed means you're much less likely to do so.

Any annoyance you experience in yoga can be used as good practice; once you learn to become more aware of yourself in class, you are better equipped to deal effectively with annoying experiences in your everyday life. The only problem with looking within is that you might not like what you see.

'Wow! I'm such a bitch!'

Through yoga and meditation I became better at noticing my thoughts and letting them pass, but as a consequence, I began to notice something that I really wasn't expecting; that I wasn't a very nice person. In fact, I might even go as far to say that I was a bit of a bitch.

I shouldn't have been so surprised; one friend did once tell me, 'I like you because you're bitchy', which wasn't the best compliment I'd ever received, but at the time I didn't take it too seriously. Sure, I liked a good old bitch and a gossip but didn't everybody? And as we've already seen, one of my major problems in life was being too nice, so I couldn't have been that bad.

But the more I began to notice my thoughts and emotions, the less I liked what I saw. Every time a colleague made a mistake, I'd verbally rip them to pieces behind their back or if I was really ticked off, take great pleasure in telling them off in person, making sure they knew just how angry I was.

Whenever I heard any hint of gossip, I'd be eager to join in, and as much as I tried, I couldn't control my temper. Every time I snapped at someone for something insignificant I'd tell myself I'd never do it again. I'd tell myself I shouldn't be like that; that I was too spiritual for all that now; I should know better. But sometimes just minutes later, I'd be at it again.

Even if I did refrain from losing my temper or criticising someone, I'd notice how much I wanted to do it. How much I wanted to be right. I felt terribly guilty, but no matter how hard I tried, I couldn't stop wanting to criticise.

Sometimes, I felt it would be easier to go back to the way I was before; I was miserable, but at least in the past I had the satisfaction of knowing it was everybody else's fault and that I was always right.

This time I didn't have that luxury; I knew it was wrong

to complain about my colleague who was always off work. I knew it was wrong to make fun of my students' English in the staffroom, but even if I didn't do it out loud, I wanted to. I *really* wanted to.

What was wrong with me? Why couldn't I stop myself? Why was I such a bitch?

Remember that the mind doesn't like it when your start to take back control of your life and it will do all it can to stay in charge. So when you make a mistake, it will take great pleasure in telling you that you've failed. Therefore, when I lost my temper or wanted to put someone down, my mind would tell me I was no good and there was no point in trying to change anymore. That I was a bitch and that's all there was to it.

Don't judge yourself harshly for thinking the way you do or for losing your temper because if you were to beat yourself up about it, that would mean you were now only doing to yourself what you've been doing to another person. Remember to just be glad that you've noticed. The more frequently you are aware of your negative tendencies, the more distance you will create between thought and action. More space will then be created between you and your thoughts. Then the thoughts will decrease in power, and the negative tendencies will subside.

Being constantly faced with yourself is tough. It's like having a permanent mirror held up to your face which is designed to show you how ugly you are. You may even be tempted to chuck the whole thing in and go back to 'normal'. But be grateful for that mirror; it tells you what you need to do to become the person you really are underneath the negativity.

Sometimes, however, the confusion about your thoughts and the temptation to judge yourself harshly may contribute to one of the most worrying aspects of yoga:

*

Thinking your teacher is the Dalai Lama in disguise

When you've had enough of your life as it is; when you know something has to change and you don't quite know what to do about it, it's natural to want to turn to someone to show you the way forward. Your yoga teacher may seem like the obvious choice; they seem calm and serene, comfortable in their own skin; they may appear to be the very person you want to become. As a student, especially if you lack confidence, it's easy to fall into the trap of feeling that you're inferior to them, and that you need them to fix what you perceive to be wrong with your life.

One thing I really feel should be addressed more in yoga classes is the emotional side of the practice. When I first attended, I thought I'd stick my legs up in the air and go home. I didn't know I'd be getting all emotional and confused, I didn't know I'd feel teary-eyed at the end of a class, I didn't know the way I felt about my life would change.

The yoga postures can help to release emotions that have been stuck in our bodies for years. While this is a good thing, when this happens, what often occurs is the process of transference, in which the emotions released are directed onto your teacher and you begin to think that they are responsible for the powerful changes that are happening in your life. It's not uncommon for students to start holding their teachers up to be some 'enlightened' being (Horton, 2011).

Fortunately for me, I was curious enough about my feelings to do my own research in this area as soon as I began to feel confused about the emotions that were coming up in class, so I was able to see what was happening and separate my feelings from any of my teachers relatively quickly, but from the reading I'd done and from talking to other yoga teachers and students, I know that some aren't so lucky; it can take much longer for them to understand what's happening and they may even get taken advantage of by a teacher who – consciously or unconsciously – wants to be seen as someone 'special' (Horton, 2011).

It's so easy to fall into the trap of thinking your teacher is too spiritual or enlightened to be trying to take advantage of your adoration, but we need to remember that these people are human, and that they are on the same path of self-awareness as you. At one point, they would most probably have been in the same position as you. It's going to be tough for them not to be affected by a room full of students hanging on to every word they say.

Over the past year or so I've read several stories of blatant abuse by yoga teachers, but there are also times when their behaviour is not so obviously sinister; adjustments that were bordering on intimate but not quite sexual, eye-contact that goes on for a bit too long, prolonged lectures about the meaning of life.

When you're new to a practice like yoga, and you start to feel uncomfortable with something that's happening, it's easy to ignore your own instinct because you feel inferior to your teacher and think that maybe you just don't 'get it'.

But the truth is that we can't always rely on the teacher to behave professionally, as much as we should be able to. Students need to keep themselves safe.

Speak up if you feel uncomfortable (or leave)

Deep down, you know if something doesn't feel right. So speak up if you're feeling uncomfortable with a touch or something your teacher is saying or doing. When all's said and done, it doesn't really matter if you *are* being paranoid; if you're not happy, leave.

This doesn't mean you can't still take responsibility for your part in the situation – I still had to accept that I relied too much on other people and was falling into people-pleaser territory again by not wanting to question my teachers – but you can still address those issues once you're out of the situation. Keeping yourself safe isn't running away; it's the sensible thing to do.

Be your own teacher

I once told a friend about a meditation class that I thought was amazing. 'What was it that you found so useful?' he asked me. I was stumped for an answer. I didn't know what to say; I suddenly realised that my teacher hadn't said anything that I didn't already know. His words had acted merely as a guide for applying this knowledge to certain areas of my life. However, in reality I hadn't needed his class to know what he was saying was true.

You don't need any particular teacher or guru; in fact, you'll find most of the teachings say the same thing after a while anyway, and if you begin to get attached to any one teacher, you start to miss the whole point. You don't become more 'you', you become more 'them.'

Go to your classes, read your books and listen to your CDs, but don't become dependent. Learn to listen to and trust yourself.

Take care of yourself in your yoga classes and you'll find that it will take you in a direction that you would never have considered before. You'll feel healthier, more confident and more able to tackle what life throws at you. A regular practice can have serious benefits for your life. Once you've managed to wade through the bullshit, you'll find a way that will lead to a happier and calmer you.

7

Stop Following the Flock, Follow Your Dream Instead

The older I've got, the more I find conversation revolves around three main topics; work, houses, and having a family. It seems everybody wants a promotion, everybody wants to be married with children, everyone wants to be on the property ladder, and when these things don't happen by a certain time we start to panic. We feel depressed because we think we've failed. We look to those who have it all and we're jealous. We wonder where it all went wrong for us.

Well, I say we, but actually for a long time I was mostly unaware that I'd failed to stick to life's schedule. I'd managed as far as being born and going to school and university, but after that I lost the timetable and didn't even notice, which was just as well really because I was usually depressed enough as it was.

My ignorance was probably thanks to working in EFL, an industry which is full of people my age and older with few or no responsibilities. When I returned to live in England, however, the realisation that I was 'lagging behind' gradually began to creep up on me. I'd be asked if I was interested in becoming a 'proper' teacher at a state school, and be met with puzzled looks when I said 'no'. Increasingly, I'd be asked why I wasn't married. I didn't know what to say; I mean, I *wanted* to get married, but hadn't realised there was a deadline. I'd hear people complaining about the difficulties of getting on the property ladder and wondered if I was strange for not being bothered.

In the summer of 2011, I decided the answer was 'yes'. I was thirty-three years old, I needed to start climbing the career ladder, take some responsibilities and plan for my future. I needed to grow up. I still had no desire to be a 'proper' teacher, but an opportunity came up at work to go for the job of Senior Teacher for the summer, with the possibility of continuing afterwards. I was delighted when they said I could have the job; responsibility, a better salary, a company T-shirt and hoodie – I was on my way! Next up was looking for a place of my own. A bigger income meant I was in with a chance of getting a mortgage. Me? A homeowner? I couldn't believe it. Suddenly, I felt all grown up.

Until I actually went to see the places in my price range; I didn't want any of them. Usually they were in dodgy areas and they always had that abomination of modern living, the open-plan living-room and kitchen. I went to an estate agent to discuss mortgages and ended up just listening because I had no idea what the woman was on about. I tried to nod occasionally to give the impression I understood, but I'm not sure it worked. The one thing I did understand was that I'd be spending all my money and probably borrowing a whole lot more just for the pleasure of borrowing even more money from a bank. Did I really want to do that? To buy a living room with a cooker in it?

At the same time, I was becoming disillusioned with Senior Teacher life; I was working most of the time in an office, which was what I'd become a teacher to escape from in the first place. I'd be exhausted after a stressful day at work, with little time in the evening to relax. Most of the time I was irritated with someone; colleagues, students, housemates, myself. I didn't want to be grown-up anymore! This wasn't any fun at all!

Eventually, the situation was resolved when I found a beautiful flat to rent by myself, much bigger than the ones I'd looked into buying, and went back to being 'just' a teacher. I was much happier that way, and I even got to keep the T-shirt and hoodie. But I couldn't help thinking, *I've failed at this grown up stuff. Why don't I want the things everybody else thinks I should? Is there something wrong with me?*

Stop and ask yourself why you really want something

Around the same time as my grown-up failure, I did something I once vowed I would never, ever do.

I joined Facebook.

I'm not altogether sure what possessed me now; I possibly got fed up with being 'the odd one out', but whatever my reasons, I found myself faced with a daily stream of 'you're a loser' messages. I looked at the people I went to school and university with and my mind went into overdrive:

> What? She's married?! But nobody fancied her at school! How come she can get a bloke and I can't!? They've got their own house with a garden shed? Damn my single rented life! Oh my God! Everybody's pregnant! What if I never have a family? He's a what?! I don't even understand that job title! It must be so important and interesting. Oh, I'm such a failure.

Fortunately, another little voice in my head made itself heard amid all the internal whining. It asked me, *Do you want what they've got?*
Answer: *I don't know.*
So what's the problem, then?
I...don't know.

I stopped and asked myself what it was that was really bothering me. *Did* I want the life I was seeing on my computer screen? Well, yes and no. Ideally, I wanted to get married and have children, but I knew it wasn't a passport to happiness. I wanted my own place one day, but not with a massive mortgage; I'd rather stay in my lovely rented flat, and the thought of a career wearing a suit and working nine to five in an office makes me feel positively queasy.

Looking back, I now believe my inferiority complex came about as a result of having realised that I'd unwittingly turned my back on 'normal' life. When I'd made a half-hearted attempt to do what I was 'supposed' to do I didn't get anywhere. It wasn't so much that I'd 'fallen behind'. It was more the fact that I didn't really want to catch up but had no idea what it was I did want to do.

I realised that I wasn't normal.

Oh dear.

From observing the people around me, I have come to a controversial conclusion, which is this; nobody's normal. Look at the people around you who have everything. How many people do you know who have the job, the car, the relationship, the house and the family? Are they all happier than you? Are they all bubbling with excitement when they walk into work every morning? Do they always speak of the joy their children bring and never the problems? Have their issues of self-esteem magically disappeared? Are their lives stress-free? Probably not.

Unhappiness isn't just reserved for those who have failed to keep up with the programme. It's everywhere; few people have achieved happiness by simply ticking off everything on life's to do list. They've tried to fit themselves into some arbitrary structure of what normal looks like and when it doesn't fit, they blame their circumstances or the people in their life. They look at those who don't have it all and tell them that they should hurry up and get with the programme, in an attempt to make themselves feel better; they may not be happy, but at least they're normal, which is all that matters.

Almost everybody is doing the same; they go to work, and moan about it, they have kids and then complain about them, or they buy a house and then stress over costs of paying for it. There's always a problem. But they do nothing about it because it's normal. They should be grateful they've got a job. They should be thankful they're on the property ladder.

Really?

It seems strange to me that with something as important as your life and your own well-being, we're so easily swayed by what other people think. Just who was it who decided that the same things should make us all happy? And why do we all fall for it when the opposite is so clearly true? We blindly go through our lives struggling to achieve all the things we're told we should want. When we find that they don't bring us happiness it takes courage to step out of the 'norm' and go our own way.

Ask yourself; do you want a promotion because you think you'd enjoy the job? Or do you just think you need to climb the career ladder because you've been told you should? Do you want to get married because you really want to share your life with someone or because you're surrounded by people who've tied the knot? I'm not trying to stop anyone from progressing in their life and career; just the opposite. I'm trying to encourage you to make sure you're doing what you want and not what you think you should want. If you find it's the latter, or maybe you already have it all and are wondering why on earth you're still not happy with your life, it's time to get clear about who you really are and what you really want.

'But it's just a silly dream!'

I'd always thought I had no ambition, no idea of what I wanted to do with my life but the truth is, I knew for over a decade before I left work that I wanted to write. Like many people, I was held back by the thought that it was just a dream; of course I could see that other people had managed to publish books, but they were the exceptions. I just wasn't that sort of person. I couldn't live my dreams; that's why they were called dreams. I wasn't a go-getter, I was a get-what-I'm-given. I was average, ordinary, and ordinary people got jobs and did what they were told.

You may think that you don't know what you want to do with your life, but you'll probably find that somewhere deep within you there is *something*. Maybe you want to write books, be an actor, an adventurer, or make money out of your hobby. It's just that you've told yourself it's not possible, you aren't talented enough, or you're too old. Well, there's a reason that desire is still there. If you're still thinking that there's something you'd love to do if only you could, it's worth giving it a try.

When I left work to finish writing this book, I had no income and I was living off my savings. I had no book deal, little idea of how to self-publish and absolutely no guarantee that anyone would want to read my work. Did I ever wonder what in the world I was doing? Of course I did. Did I have an overwhelming sense of self-belief and confidence in my writing talents to see me through? Not really. Sometimes, I looked back at what I'd written and thought it was so bad that I'd be lucky if my mum bought it. I missed my colleagues, I got lonely and fearful sometimes, wondering why I'd left a job I didn't mind doing to jump into such an uncertain future.

But when I was tempted to ring my boss and ask for my job back, I knew I just couldn't. I had to *try* to make it work. I could live with trying and failing. I could no longer live with not trying at all. Taking the first step is probably the most difficult part of going for your dream. Once you've done that, you begin to realise that there really isn't such a thing as failing; with every mistake you make, you learn something, which can then be used to help you achieve what you want.

'They'll laugh at me'
So often, we're held back by the fear of what other people will think of us if we dare to tell them what we really want to do; we're scared to say we want to be rock stars or artists because it seems too 'far out.'

I wanted to try teaching EFL for about two years before I did it; I thought everyone would tell me to forget it because I was too shy and wouldn't be able to do it. I only took the plunge because someone else had suggested it to me; the fact that another person thought I might be capable meant I now had 'permission' to give it a go. And what comments did I get when I *did* sign up for the course? 'Oh, go for it. I think you'll be a good teacher.'

Unfortunately, my fears of ridicule stayed with me when I started writing. I was reluctant to tell anyone, but when I did, the most common responses were 'Good for you' or 'Ooh, sounds exciting.'

So often our fears of what people think of us are only in our heads. But supposing they do laugh at you, what then? Try to look at it as a good sign; it means you're dreaming big!

Breaking free of survival mode
When I finally made the decision to leave my job, the reaction I got from colleagues was mixed. There were those who were supportive, others were confused, and the rest told me how jealous they were. What united the majority of them was the assumption that I had a job lined up. When I told them that I didn't, the question was always, 'So, what kind of job are you looking for?' The thought

that I would be anything other than somebody else's employee never occurred to them.

That's what people like us did; we worked for other people and we worked in order to survive. Even when I told them I wanted to find a way of working for myself, I was given advice on how to make money; I could get work at the shops over Christmas or I should start looking for private students right away. What they couldn't see was that making money immediately wasn't my concern; I was lucky that I had enough in savings to keep me going for about six months. If making enough money to survive was my goal I would've just stayed where I was.

Still, it was hard to push the comments aside; I'd always been an employee and I'd always believed that we should just be grateful to have work that provides us with enough money to eat. If we are to go for our dreams, we need to start reviewing the way we see work and put what we want ahead of our basic survival instincts.

What helped me was following the advice of John Williams in *Screw Work Let's Play* (2010), in which he stresses the importance of letting go of what we believe is possible and just allowing ourselves to dream first; I imagined what I could have if money and time were not an issue; I asked myself what I would do, and have, if literally anything were possible. I created a vision board of all the things I wanted and that inspired me and stuck it in my living room to remind me of what my future held. I repeated affirmations to myself about all the things I wanted to experience. Gradually, I began to see things move into the direction I wanted. My writing began to take more shape, I had ideas that I hadn't had before. I found teachers and resources by chance that I hadn't even heard of previously.

If you can let go of what you think is possible, and allow yourself to imagine what your ideal life would be like, the 'hows' of the situation will become more available to you over time.

'But I've got too many responsibilities'

Some people at work would tell me how they wished they could leave, but they had bills to pay, they had mouths to feed or their partner would kill them. These were valid points; I *was* lucky that I had the time and money to pursue my dream, and that nobody was depending on me to earn an income, but having responsibilities needn't stop you. You don't have to leave your job or wait until the kids have left home before taking your first steps towards your dream. And if you're feeling overwhelmed by fear, I certainly wouldn't recommend quitting your job. You need to be in the right frame of mind before taking such a leap.

Start by taking small steps; read an article about what you want to do, book a class, talk to someone doing the same thing or start a blog. However small it is, take some action each day. If you do this, you'll get there eventually, and you're likely to find that your current life is that much more enjoyable in the meantime. I'd been writing for eight months before I left my job, and during that time I found I began to enjoy work much more because I had that creative outlet when I got home. It was only when the book needed more attention and I had exhausted myself trying to do both that I realised it was time to leave the day job.

Where work and money is concerned, other people will always offer you an opinion, whether you want it or not. When you start to step outside the 'norm', you may find that your friends and family can't support you in the way you'd like. They want to see that you're settled and safe; they want to know you have enough money to pay the bills and it may seem like they're talking sense. After all, the bills won't pay themselves and initially at least, you will obviously have more financial security in your regular day job. But is it really worth it if you're suppressing who you really are and what's important to you?

You may find you need to distance yourself from your family or friends, at least in that area of your life, and surround yourself with other people who understand your need to break away from what's 'normal.' If you can't find people in the real world, there will always be someone online who is going through the same thing. Thanks to the internet, we can always find someone that can offer a word of encouragement or who can simply tell you that they understand.

'But I really do want the house, the family, etc…'
Perhaps you've decided normal life really *is* for you. Maybe you've looked into your heart and decided that is what you want; you want the good job, you want to be married with kids and live in a big house. Well, apart from the job, that's what I want too. But taking steps to do the work I love has helped me to see that what I want *is* possible, and I don't need to look at other people and feel bad that I haven't got there yet.

Resist comparing yourself to others; instead, look at how far you've come. What can you do now that you couldn't in the past? What have you achieved over the last year, no matter how small it may seem to someone from the outside? Don't judge your progress by where another person is in their life.

Remember that one day, you'll die
Sorry to break it to you like that, but it's true. The only thing we don't know is when. Like most people, I used to find this a scary thought, but now I look at it differently.

When I look back on my life, I'm pretty horrified by the amount of time I've spent worrying about doing the right thing, what people thought of me and crying over not having this or that. It's like looking at a different person now. I imagine sometimes how sad it would have been if I'd spent my entire life like that and ended up lying on my deathbed with nothing but misery to look back on.

Now that I'm fully invested in running my own race and following my dreams it no longer matters if they don't come true; it's the process of working towards them that is making me happy and giving me life. In reality, it doesn't matter if I run out of money and nobody wants this book, or if I never get married and have children. In the end I'll go the same way as everyone else and I can say I've had fun along the way.

So search your own heart and find what's normal for you. When you do this, you'll find you're free to embrace life and all its possibilities. Only then will you discover what you're truly capable of.

8

Start Trusting Life

If there's a bigger waste of energy than worrying, I don't know what it is. What could be more pointless than sitting around fretting over some imaginary event in the future that you can't control and probably won't even happen? Yet there was a time, not so long ago when I could have become world champion in the Worry Olympics.

Even when I was little, I was consumed by thoughts of impending doom: *What if I fail my spelling test? What if I'm late for school?* As I got older these fears progressed to: *What if I don't get that job? What if that person doesn't like me anymore? What if I've forgotten to turn the heating off?* Or *What if I run out of money? What if...?*

When the fear of what's going to happen dominates our lives, the tendency is often to try and control the outcome in some way; working harder than necessary to guarantee success; waking up much earlier than needed to make sure we're on time; applying for any old job just so we'll get *one*; checking the heating has been turned off ten times before we leave the house; or not even putting the heating on because we're so afraid of how much the gas bill will be.

Considering my own history of worrying, it's surprising that today, living mostly off my savings with no regular income,

I feel remarkably self-assured. Sure, there's been a couple of meltdowns along the way, but most of the time I've been pretty relaxed about the money situation; almost to the extent that I tell myself I *should* be worrying more. I *should* be working harder to get published and start earning.

But I just can't; I work at an unhurried pace, taking breaks when needed. Sometimes I get a fair amount done. Sometimes I write next to nothing. And yet by the end of my first month of freedom, I'd already beaten the three month deadline I'd set myself for getting the second draft of this book finished.

So what's going on? How can I be in such a precarious situation, with no guarantee of success, work at such a lazy pace and yet still get more work done than I'd originally planned to do? And how can I not worry about my ever-decreasing savings?

What's changed is that I now have a deep trust that everything will be OK.

How?

If you want to stop stressing out and worrying about how everything will turn out, a good way to start is to accept that there is something more going on in the universe than just random life forms being born and doing random acts before dropping dead.

If you think otherwise, just look at the world around you. Look at how each creature on Earth is adapted to its environment, how our bodies automatically know what to do, or how the seasons come and go. Coincidence? Scientific accident? Really? How likely this that?

We trust we're going to have air to breathe every day and we trust the planet will continue to turn but we don't trust we'll get to work on time or that we'll still be alive if we don't.

*

Still not convinced? Look for evidence in your own life

Almost two years ago I was given notice on the house I was sharing with three others. I wasn't upset because I was already thinking about finding somewhere else to live by myself. But now I had a deadline by which to find somewhere, which made me slightly nervous. I knew finding accommodation in Bournemouth wouldn't be hard, but I didn't just want to live *anywhere;* I wanted a place where I could stay long-term. I had an image of the flat I wanted in my mind; it simply HAD to have a separate kitchen and living room, and would preferably have room for a dining table and chairs, and maybe even have the odd character fireplace.

On my budget, that wasn't going to be an easy find. I actually spent only three weeks looking, but it felt like three years. Almost everywhere I went was open-plan, even when they had masses of hallway space and two bedrooms. I was exasperated; why have all that space and then have only one room for the two most important rooms of the house? The few that did manage to separate the two were either tiny or in dodgy areas or both.

Eventually, as the moving date neared, I began to accept that I might have to give up. I went to see one flat that I thought I could live with; it had tiny living space with a kitchen attached but there was also a big bedroom and hallway. It was nice, modern and clean. *Yes, perhaps I could compromise*, I told myself as I made my way home.

Then, once I got back online, I saw it; I literally screamed at the computer screen, 'That's my flat!' It had it all; separate living room and kitchen, a big bedroom, and even a couple of character fireplaces. Plus it was cheaper than nearly all the flats I'd already seen. And it was just over the road from where I was already living!! I couldn't believe my luck, especially when I actually went for a viewing and found that it was even bigger than it looked online. It was almost as though God was saying, 'Oh yeah, sorry, I forgot, I've got this one. Any good?'

This is a relatively small example, but when you begin to see the universe helping you out in small ways, you can learn to have faith that it will help you out with the bigger picture.

How many times have you been about to give up on something, only to have it all work out at the last minute? Or have you ever been worried sick about something happening and have it all turn out fine? Maybe it all went wrong but it actually wasn't as bad as you thought. Or maybe it really was a complete disaster but it helped you become a stronger person. Things are always working out for the best in one way or another.

Don't confuse trust with being passive or lazy

Often when we hear religious folks telling us we just have to believe, or advocates of the Law of Attraction telling us we just need to think our way to what we want, we too easily dismiss what they say. 'I can imagine £1 million in my bank account but it's not going to make the money get there', is an argument I've heard time and time again, but it's a misunderstanding of the message of believing all things are possible.

Of course you have to do something to make your desires and dreams come true, or to have a problematic situation work out, but the point is if you relax and have faith in *something*, whether you call it God, the universe, a higher power or whatever, the answers will come to you much more easily than if you're panicking, over analysing, drawing up lists of pros and cons and asking everybody and their dog what you should do.

For years I tried to control my external world; I tried to plan everything, mostly around how much money I'd make.

I remember when I was in New Zealand, I had very little money left after my time in Australia, so I spent the whole holiday applying for jobs online so I knew I'd have something lined up for when I got back. By that stage I really wanted to work in England, but knowing how hard it would be to get EFL work here, I started applying in any country that sounded OK. Financially it worked out, but I was so stressed out that I didn't enjoy the holiday at all and hated the job I eventually found in Italy; I was so intent on getting *a* job I hadn't even thought about getting one I'd actually enjoy.

Once I stopped stressing out and started to trust that everything would be all right, I found that life became much more helpful towards me; I got the job in England I'd wanted for years, I found a great place to live, I effortlessly saved enough money to eventually leave work to pursue my dream and was able to get on with my writing even though I had no idea when I would have an income again. Of course I had to take action to make all these things happen, but the first step was in believing they were all possible and that it would happen *somehow*. When I truly began to believe that, the *how* became clearer to me more quickly than it had in the past.

Decisions, decisions

Do you find it difficult to make decisions? What do you do to help you decide? Talk to family and friends? Google your problem? Write a list of pros and cons? Toss a coin?

I've often struggled to make decisions, and have tried all of these methods in the hope that one of them will say to me, 'Yes, this is what you must do, and when you do it, everything will work out exactly as you'd like.'

What has been the most useful method? Believe it or not, tossing a coin, because I know immediately if it lands on the 'wrong' one. The disappointment or relief I feel when I see the result tells me what I should do, which is always what I wanted to do anyway.

Have I made poor choices in my life? Yes.

Has my life been irreparably ruined as a result? No.

Have I learned from my mistakes? Yes.

So why am I still afraid of making one? I don't know.

We all want to avoid pain, yet it can be through some of our most painful experiences that we grow. If we are to become the strongest people that we can be, if we are to achieve everything we are meant to achieve, we have to learn to trust our intuition. We need to follow what our gut is telling us, which often doesn't seem like the most sensible option. Leaving my job to write wasn't sensible, but it was what my gut was telling me to do. It may yet lead me into some difficult situations, but the challenges we face in life are what help us to grow and what in turn give us the confidence we need to face every situation thrown at us.

However, even when you know this, there will likely be one thing that still confuses you: fear.

When should we ignore fear?

For a while, I was confused about fear; we're told we should face our fears if we're going to become our best selves and yet fear has stopped me making what would have been some very silly decisions.

It seems to me that there are two types of fear. One is where your gut is telling you 'NO!', while the other is your mind saying, 'Ooh, are you sure about this?' It's important to learn the difference between the two.

When I first began writing, I was doing a correspondence course which encouraged its students to try to get their work published while they studied. My tutor said that she'd enjoyed my second assignment and recommended I sent it off to my target magazine in the hope that they'd publish it. Of course, I was pleased that she thought it was good, but as I sat down to rewrite it, something held me back. I told myself that I was just being silly, that I was scared of rejection and I should just give it a go, but every time I thought about doing so, I just couldn't. I had a gut feeling that was screaming, 'Don't do it!'

Shortly afterwards, I wrote a piece for the website *Tiny Buddha*. It was quite a personal piece, and if accepted would appear with my name and photo next to it. This was a terrifying prospect for someone so private who until then had only posted online anonymously. Thoughts about the possible consequences of being so exposed and possibly having my work criticised raced through my mind. Nevertheless, I sent the article because despite the fear, it felt like the right thing to do.

Likewise, when I first took my letter of resignation into work in early 2013, something told me not to give it to my boss. I was fed up with work at the time, annoyed about some changes that had taken place, and didn't think much of the new boss, but when it came to giving him the letter, I couldn't bring myself to do it. It felt wrong. About five months later, work had improved; my old boss had returned from maternity leave, making the atmosphere much more pleasant, and things were generally more relaxed. But I knew I had to leave. I was still nervous about taking such a big step and a big risk, but as with the *Tiny Buddha* article, it felt right; scary, but right.

It was through experiences such as these that I began to understand the difference between the fear you should listen to and the fear that you need to push through to get where you want to be. When something just feels wrong, you know it.

Trust that feeling.

Learning to take more notice of how your body reacts to certain situations will help you become better able to know what action is right for you.

Don't rush

Unless you have a decision that needs to be made this instant, you can afford to take your time. If you're wondering whether to leave a job or a partner, or move house, there's rarely a deadline you have to stick to, so let the situation go for a while and eventually there'll come a time when you'll know what to do.

Sleep on it, for a few days, weeks or even months. If you still want to do something, then you should probably go ahead and do it (if for no other reason than just making a decision!).

Leaving my job was the most difficult decision I've had to make recently. I had the feeling that I had to leave about a year before I did so. For so many months the only question wasn't 'if' but 'when'. I wasn't planning to get another job so the uncertainty frightened me. *Should I wait until I'm a published author? How much longer will it take to write anything decent if I stay? Maybe I should stay until my summer holiday? Or the end of the current lease on my flat? Where will I live if I have to move out?*

I remember calling out to God and saying, 'Look, if you're up there just tell me what to do'. I wasn't asking for a sign. I wanted Him to just come down with His big white beard and tell me, 'You must hand in your notice on Monday morning and I promise you everything will work out perfectly. And take in a Victoria sponge on your last day.' But He didn't. Maybe He was busy.

Eventually, I got fed up with asking and let it go. Only then did the answer come to me. When I felt seriously depressed about the thought of going back to work after a holiday (a feeling I'd never had in connection to that job before, even when things weren't going well), I knew that it was time for me to leave.

Don't listen to people who don't know what they're talking about

When it comes to your life and particularly the choices you have to make, you've probably found that everybody else knows exactly what you should do and is very keen to tell you, whether you've asked for their opinion or not. The problem with this is that they can't possibly know what's right for you, even if they've been in that situation themselves, because they're not you. They haven't lived your life; they don't know your story. They're looking at things from *their* perspective and what is right for them may not necessarily be right for you.

Deep down, we always know what we want to do, so we don't need to ask the advice of all our family and friends. Our hearts may not lead us down the easiest of roads but sometimes we just need to take a big leap of faith and trust that everything will be all right. And when we do that, one way or another, it will be.

Learning to relax and trust that things will work out has improved my life dramatically. It's not that I'm falsely optimistic or that I'm convinced that riches are coming my way. I'm just no longer afraid of failure. I know I'm going to get what I need in life. As a result, I'm much calmer; I hardly worry about anything anymore. This more relaxed state of mind has increased my levels of creativity and I find it much easier to make decisions, knowing that I am able to handle whatever happens next.

9

Beware of the 'C' Word

Since I began practising yoga and meditation, one word that has invaded my energy field more than any other is the 'C' word.

No! Not *that* one! Although the one I'm talking about is rapidly becoming equally offensive to me. The 'C' word I'm referring to is 'connect.'

We don't make friends anymore; we connect. We don't have a chat; we connect. Even leaving comments on a blog means we've somehow made a deep soul connection with its founder that can never be broken. We're encouraged to hug each other, stare into each other's eyes, hold hands and share our feelings. All in the name of the 'C' word.

Don't get me wrong; I understand the need for all this. I am fully aware of the human need for connection to others. I've even bought books in an attempt to improve my abilities in this area. I read them as well; that's how dedicated I am. The real problem I have with the continuous use of the 'C' word is that it's a constant reminder that I'm a bit crap at it.

It's always taken me longer than others to make good friends, but somehow the 'C' word seems to make me feel worse. Every time I hear it, I'm reminded of how difficult I find it to form close relationships. Everybody else seems to be better at it than me. Am I the only one who gets freaked out by intense eye contact in a yoga class? Am I a freak because I prefer to make sure someone wants to be hugged before I fling my arms round them? How come all the people around me can connect and I can't? Am I destined to be alone forever?

Considering the amount of material out there advising us on how to connect with others, I can only assume that in fact, it isn't just me; if it were, everyone would just be getting on with their fabulous relationships and I wouldn't be hearing the 'C' word so often. I'd be left in peace to sit on my own in my own connection free world. Therefore, the aims of this chapter are to help take the pressure off any other connection-phobes out there who may also be feeling inadequate and to share what has helped me in taking my first baby steps towards more fulfilling friendships.

If you've got no friends, the first step is fairly easy, at least on a practical level.

Spend some time alone

Paradoxically, we need to be comfortable being with ourselves if we want to form a real connection with others. After all, if *you* don't like being with you, how can you expect anyone else to enjoy your company? When I was at college, I used to have loads of friends, but I still felt lonely. I felt nobody really cared about me or understood me. My distance from them likely came from the fact that I wasn't really being me when I was with them, I was being who I thought I had to be to fit in. But of course I didn't realise that then; I just blamed everyone around me. I felt constantly disappointed by my friends, and I entered each new friendship I with the hope that this would be the one person I'd be able to count on and who would be my friend forever. What a pressure to put on someone!

This pattern continued right up until I was thirty, when

I was left without any friends in Poland. I've already spoken about how it allowed me to understand myself better, but it also taught me to enjoy spending time on my own.

Eventually, my loneliness turned into solitude. I began to take time to do things for myself; I learned to cook decent meals and read books I found interesting or that would help me to grow. In time, I began to go outwards; attending dance classes, then eventually moving on to yoga. In time, I was fine whether I went out or not or had company or not. I was happy in either case.

You don't need to have as dramatic an introduction to solitude as mine to learn how to be by yourself. You can take a little time each day just to be alone. Really alone. This is another reason why meditation is helpful; it gives you time to sit in silence with no TV, radio, or internet to distract you from your loneliness.

When you learn to enjoy your own company, you no longer feel that you need your friends to make you feel like a worthwhile person. You don't cling to any one person hoping that they'll never let you down. Then you can actually just enjoy being with them.

Know what you have to offer

When you suffer from low self-esteem, it's easy to think that you should wait for the other person to make the first move. Maybe you don't invite people to spend time with you or you don't want to 'bother' them. It still takes me some effort to make the first move in social situations. *Should I text so-and-so? Should I invite them round? Maybe they won't want to come? What if they don't enjoy being with me?*

Again, spending time alone can help you rediscover what interests you and what you have to offer. Can you cook? Maybe you could invite a friend or colleague round for dinner. Are you particularly knowledgeable in a specific area? Perhaps you could offer your expertise. Everybody has something that they can offer another person.

Think of all your good qualities; write them down if you need to. Knowing what you have to offer another person will help you to see how lucky others will be to have you in their life. Using meditations with affirmations has helped me considerably. Many are available online that can be listened to while you are falling asleep. Hearing the words over and over will help turn your subconscious mind around and you'll become more accustomed to thinking in a positive way.

Know that other people are also scared

Often we look at other people and feel inferior in comparison. It never used to occur to me that others had the same problems as me. If I saw someone more outgoing or talkative than me, I took that as a sign of confidence, never stopping to think that perhaps this person also felt lonely.

What I've learned over the last year or so is that essentially, we're all the same; we are all scared, get lonely, suffer from self-doubt and we all have different ways of coping.

This knowledge has helped me to become less fearful of making the first move to contact someone and less afraid of rejection. In reality you don't know why somebody doesn't want to spend time with you. Maybe they don't like you, or maybe the problem is that *they* feel inferior to *you*.

Remember, we don't know what is going on in another person's head, but I can guarantee you that more likely than not, it's filled with a mess equal to that in yours and mine. We all have issues, we're all weird in our own way, nobody is perfect, no-one has it all sorted out.

Know your boundaries

I think part of what annoys me so much about the overuse of the 'C' word is that to me it implies that we *should* be doing something more than we are already. Each one of us starts this personal development stuff from a different place. Some people feel comfortable sharing their problems; some might be fine with a hug from a stranger while others will find that threatening or weird.

I remember doing a workshop where we each had to choose a reading from a collection of passages and poems and say why they resonated with us. I didn't particularly like any of them and didn't want to speak in front of the group. Looking back, I probably should have said so; I'd paid for the weekend and had every right not to do something I didn't want to do. But I did it. I chose a poem; made up some rubbish about why I'd picked it and nervously spoke to the group about my ideas.

Did I feel better for facing the challenge? No; it set me back a little as I stressed over whether I sounded stupid or said the wrong thing. (Of course, I now realise that they were probably too preoccupied with their own talk to worry about me. I can't remember a word of what the rest of the group said and I'm sure it's the same for each of them.)

We need to challenge ourselves; we need to break out of our comfort zones, otherwise none of us would ever do anything. But know what feels doable for you at that time; don't allow yourself to be pushed into something you really don't feel you could try right now. Go at a pace that feels right for you.

One of the areas that has concerned me slightly is the issue of touch. All I've been hearing over the last year or so is that we need to touch and be touched. Well it's true, but the harsh reality is that not everybody wants to be touched by everybody else. I know we're all one and we're all supposed to love each other, but like it or not, it's a fact that some people repel us while others don't. I like a hug, but it depends who's hugging me. One person's touch can be warm and reassuring, while another's can feel threatening or just irritating.

I used to work for a boss who had a habit of grabbing my arm when he spoke to me. Not the worst thing that can happen, I'll admit, but I didn't feel the need to be manhandled in such a way whenever we were speaking. It also represented to me how the power balance was in his favour; had I walked into his office and grabbed him by the arm or slapped him on the back I'm not sure he would've been best pleased.

As unspiritual as it is for me to say it, touch can be used as a power tool against another person and when we're always being told to connect it can be confusing for people in yoga classes or other 'spiritual' situations to know if someone is being creepy or if the problem is that they're not as comfortable with touch as they feel they should be.

Maybe we should all be hugging each other freely and treating everyone like they're our brothers and sisters but it's not all going to happen all at once. Different people have different comfort levels where touch is concerned, for a variety of reasons, and if they decide to step out of those comfort zones, they need to be able to do so at a pace at which they can cope, not thrown into situations where they feel panicky or uneasy so that it knocks their confidence further.

If you feel uncomfortable or that you're being pushed into doing something you really don't want to do, don't be afraid to speak up and voice your concerns.

Take it step by step

When I first realised I had difficulties in sharing my thoughts and feelings, I felt like I had to do it with everybody. This made me feel uncomfortable, but *hey!* I thought, *that's the whole point, isn't it?*

Well, maybe. As I said above, it's good to push ourselves out of our comfort zones, but not to the point where it's counterproductive.

The trouble is in knowing how much to share and with whom. We've all met people who tell us all the gory details about their sex life or tell us all their problems within five minutes of meeting us. It feels awkward and embarrassing. I didn't want to be that kind of person but nor did I want to stay the way I was; afraid to tell anybody anything about myself through fear of rejection.

The problem for me was learning what an appropriate amount to tell the other person was. When I told people something about myself, I worried that I'd shared too much; did the other person feel uncomfortable? If I kept quiet instead of speaking up, I'd be angry with myself afterwards for 'failing'.

As always, go easy on yourself. It takes time to change. Start by telling people a little about yourself and see their reaction. When you see that they're not laughing at you or rejecting you, it will help to boost your confidence in sharing more information about yourself. If you find the reaction is negative, don't take it personally; in fact a bit of rejection can be a good thing. We learn that not everybody can like us and the world doesn't end as a result.

And what about your dreams?

One of the biggest tests I had to face recently in the sharing area was that of telling people about my dreams and ambitions. Initially I kept my writing aspirations to myself, which was easy when I was working, but when I left I was faced with a dilemma; do I tell people what I'm up to and face ridicule or do I tell them I'm not doing anything and let them think I'm a lazy no-hoper?

I've heard conflicting opinions on whether it's a good idea to tell people your dreams, but I think the best approach is to simply be selective about who you tell.

Now, I tell people according to what I think their reaction might be; if they're a cynical person, I keep it to myself; I can't be bothered with the negativity. If they're more open-minded, I might tell them. Just before leaving work, I wrote about my plans in answer to another person's blog post. It's funny how I struggled to tell some members of my own family and yet had no problem in telling potentially millions of people on the internet.

If you feel that telling people your dreams will help you make them come true, do that. If you feel it will only cause you added stress and therefore prevent them from coming true, keep them to yourself for now. Everybody is different; some will crumble and give up in the face of negativity from doubters and naysayers; others will find it makes them more determined to keep going and prove everybody wrong.

Only you know yourself. Only you know your situation; do what feels right for you. Don't share your dreams because someone has told you that you should. I have found that my willingness to tell people my goals in life has increased naturally as I've gained confidence.

Find a way that works for you

Speaking doesn't come easily to me, but writing is another matter. When I had my first piece of work published on the *Tiny Buddha* website, the best thing about it was reading the comments on how much I'd helped people by sharing my story. Initially, I'd been afraid that I'd talked about myself too much, but it seemed that by daring to be open about my feelings I'd helped other people feel less alone.

That gave me the courage to continue to be more open.

I started leaving more comments on forums with my name and photo attached, whereas before I'd only ever posted anonymously. I realised that as I hadn't actually met them, there was hardly going to be a deep and meaningful bond, but this step forward helped me to eventually became more comfortable with sharing in 'real life'. Letting others know that you understand how they feel not only helps them but can do a lot to help you feel less detached.

It's still a struggle for me at times, but it's getting easier and doing it through writing first has helped. If you'd told me a few years ago that I'd be writing a book telling everybody about my fears and life experiences I would never have believed you. And yet here I am.

Smile at everybody you meet

I'm not a naturally smiley person. And when I'm not smiling I have a very miserable-looking face. However, as I've become happier in my life and less troubled by worrying and negative thoughts I have found that I've begun smiling more naturally, including times when there's nothing particularly smile-inducing going on. And when you meet new people, smiling can go a long way, especially if you're like me and you don't always feel like talking. When you're shy or nervous, other people may think you're being aloof. Smiling at people when you meet them at least says that you're open to friendship, and that you're not deliberately being stand-offish.

Listen

Have you ever said something to another person only to receive a reply that shows they've not been listening to a word you've said? They looked like they were listening; their eyes were open and facing you, perhaps they even nodded in a few places, but when it came to their turn to speak it was clear that mentally, they'd been miles away. Or that they'd already made up their mind what they were going to say and your turn was just a formality that was getting in the way of them voicing their opinion. Perhaps even worse are those who don't even pretend to listen. You're in the middle of saying something and they go, 'Ooh look at that bird over there,' making you feel really valued and appreciated.

I've always thought of myself as a good listener, but recently I've begun to question whether there's room for improvement. I've heard several times over the past couple of years that most of us are not fully listening when talking to another person; we're thinking about what to say next, or maybe even thinking about how to make a quick getaway.

When someone is speaking, listen to what they're saying. Really listen. Let the person speak; give them your undivided attention. When you've truly listened and actually heard what the other person has said, if an answer is needed it should come to you more easily and will certainly be more appropriate than any you might have thought of while they were talking.

Do something to help another person

Give your unwanted clothes to charity, help someone at work, pick up the tenner that person in front of you dropped (and then give it back to them). Think about when someone last did something to help you; didn't it make you feel all fuzzy inside? Someone cared enough to make life that little bit easier for you and I'm willing to bet you thought something along the lines of *Aw, at least there are some nice people around.*

Even if you can't see the results of your actions (for example, when giving to charity) the act of giving itself helps to bring more purpose to your life. Ironically, when we start to give without any expectations attached, that's when we start receiving.

If you use every day as an opportunity to look for ways to take tiny steps towards forming a connection, gradually, it will get easier. But above all, don't beat yourself up for not being as open or huggy-huggy as you've been told to be. You're doing your best and that's all any of us can do.

10

Challenges of Going through 'The Change'

So far, I've told you how I've learned to accept myself; that I'm no longer desperate for a boyfriend, I meditate every day, do yoga, and I now have a deep trust in the powers of the universe. Life should be easy-peasy now, right?

Well, not quite. While my life is nowadays much improved, there are times when I feel like I'm on an excruciatingly slow roller-coaster; the route is full of ups and downs and twists and turns but unlike any other roller-coaster, I can get off at any time. And I do have moments when this seems like the easiest option; when I think that perhaps I should just chuck out the yoga mat, burn all my books, go back to work and return to watching TV or getting drunk all evening. I should go back to blaming others for all my problems, to bitching about the people I don't like, to crying about how terrible and frustrating my life is.

Only I *can't* just get off this roller coaster. No matter how easy and tempting it seems at times, I'm stuck. I've already gone too far along the road and now there's no going back. When you first begin to see that there's another way to live; when you see the importance of taking responsibility for your life and that you can change it for the better, the world starts to seem a more promising place. There's hope; you find a new way of seeing things, you meet lots of interesting people and listen to all kinds of inspiring talks. You realise that no, you don't have to struggle, you don't have to be unhappy and yes, you do have a choice.

So you keep going, you're fascinated by the new things you're learning, excited to be doing new things and meeting new people and you're over the moon when life begins to take a turn for the better. Then somewhere along the line you start to feel lost.

Suddenly, you find you can't speak to your friends anymore; drunken nights out have lost their appeal and you can no longer pretend to be outraged that Susan's mother-in-law gave her kids fish fingers for tea without asking her first. Maybe, like me, your job no longer makes any sense, but you have no clue as to what you'll do instead. You start to question old habits and behaviour patterns; you don't act in a way your friends and family expect anymore. Your old life no longer fits you, but you're not too sure about your new one either.

Yes, trying to become the best person possible can be tough. We say we want to change, we say we want our lives to improve, but this requires letting go of the old you and as we're creatures of habit, it's easier said than done.

In my own experience I've had the following areas of difficulty while going through 'the change':

Friendships

When I first began practising yoga and meditation and reading all my deep and meaningful self-help books, I made the classic mistake of thinking I knew it all, and what's more that my friends would be most grateful to me for passing my superior knowledge on to them and helping them resolve all their problems in life.

I was wrong. I just pissed people off. 'Very Zen' said one friend sarcastically, after I'd tried offering her some advice. Another called me a hippy. I was mortified. I had done my best not to sound like a pretentious wannabe Zen master. Nevertheless, I had to concede that I *had* probably sounded like one. I put myself in their shoes; I remembered when I used to get all fed up and depressed over how people were treating me. There was nothing worse than being told that I could do something about it. And if you were to tell me that I should look at it from the other person's point of view, then that would be you off my Christmas card list pretty much for life. I *thought* I wanted things to change but in reality I didn't. I wanted to be angry, I wanted to vent about how unjust everything was. I wanted to blame other people and talk about how terrible they were. The last thing I wanted was some joker telling me my enemies didn't mean to hurt my feelings or that I could change the way I looked at things.

Why do we enjoy complaining and blaming others so much? Why do we want to stay angry and negative? Although we feel miserable in the 'victim' role, it does at least bring us some attention. Plus if we can get our friends to agree with how badly we've been treated, there's another advantage in that we've had confirmation that we're right in thinking the other person is a rotter. When we start suggesting to our friends that there's an alternative way of looking at things, we run the risk of preaching, as well as threatening their identity as the victim. But if we don't want to collude with them in maintaining this self-image, and they don't want to hear what we've got to say, what should we do?

Allowing people to rant when they want and not commenting either way has been one way I've tried to deal with such situations, but in a cyber-conversation that's more difficult to do. Increasingly, I've found that putting some distance between myself and these friends has been the only way to avoid being affected by their negativity. It has the added bonus of avoiding that other old vice of mine: drinking.

For years drinking was my crutch. It was my anti-shy formula that I depended on whenever I went out. Now, with the very occasional exception, I'm no longer interested in going to the pub to get drunk and my clubbing days are long gone. Added to this is the fact that since I started writing, I've noticed how much drinking affects my creativity levels the next day; my head feels foggy and my body all achy. So for the most part, I've given up drinking.

The first time I went to the pub and ordered a coke, I could hardly believe the grief I got. 'Is that just coke?' 'Why isn't there any vodka in it?' 'Why aren't you drinking?' 'I'm very disappointed, Louise.'

Faced with situations like this, I felt I no longer fitted in with my old friends, so I went in search of new ones. I began to think that maybe I should just stick to yoga people now that I'd gone all spiritual. However, when surrounded by people of the yogic world, I felt equally out of place; I didn't always understand what they were on about. I got bored with hearing the word 'energy' and fed up with not judging people. I felt confused, bored, and lonely and I just wanted to go back to 'normal.' In other words, I wanted to go to the pub, get pissed and have a good old bitch.

So that's what I tried to do. And I was bored. Again. I couldn't finish my drink and when I moaned about people, I'd feel really guilty. I now saw the pointlessness of complaining about things you're not going to do anything about. I saw that there is so much more we could be doing with our time than just sitting in pubs getting bladdered. As a result, this is the choice I was left with: pretend once again to be something I'm not for the sake of having friends or go my own way. I am lucky that I enjoy my own company. I can go for days on end without talking to anyone and it doesn't bother me. But despite this, there were still times when I thought, *Is this it, then? Am I going to be friendless for life?*

This, I have discovered, is a common problem faced by those navigating the world of self-awareness. It's something we need to go through to let go of our old selves. If you hang in there, things will improve.

Turning back isn't really an option that is open to me anymore. I may face loneliness sometimes, but it's nothing compared to that which I felt when I was younger. I can see how much my life has improved and I know I need to keep moving forward to do all the things I want to do. The key is to just relax, go with it. Some people will leave your life; others will stay and hopefully grow with you. If you are always true to yourself, if you allow yourself to have the space and time to grow and stop trying so hard to fix everybody else's life, then it will become easier to meet more people who are consistent with the new you.

Self-limiting beliefs

For most of my life, I've seen myself as a victim; bad things happened to me. Faced with new and challenging situations, I'd crumble in the hope that someone would come along and save me: my mum, my friends, or my latest imaginary boyfriend.

Leaving my job forced me to make a massive shift in my way of thinking. On the first Monday after quitting, I woke up all smug and smiley because I didn't have to go to work. I realised that whatever happened, I was already living my dream; I was a writer (albeit an unpaid one) and I would decide when and where I worked. I was free!

But just the next day I was all over the place. When I was writing, I felt I should be looking for ways to make money; when I was looking for ways to make money, I worried that I was neglecting the book and wouldn't have time to produce any decent writing. And if I dared do anything completely nonwork related, I'd feel guilty about wasting time and a little voice would come in telling me I'd never make it. *Why the hell have you left your job? it would ask me. What are you going to do now? Write a book? Do you know how many people make a living from writing? You've lost the plot. You're living in a dream world.* After a lifetime of being told what to do, I literally didn't know what to do with myself.

Part of me wanted to curl up into a little ball and give up. I wanted somebody to come in and take care of me and to sort it all out. But I knew nobody would. What's more, I know that if they had, I would've felt cheated. Leaving my job was not about becoming rich and successful but becoming a new person, shedding old habits and thought patterns that limited my life before and learning that I can look after myself.

So I ignored the thoughts and ploughed on. It took me about six weeks to feel comfortable with the routine I had developed for myself and to let go of expectations of making money; to just be grateful that I had my savings and the time to spend on producing the best work I possibly could.

Part of the difficulty in adjusting was due to the beliefs that I had formed about myself over the years; that I'm not the sort of person who works for herself, or I'm not intelligent enough to write a book or build a business. When you're so used to thinking a certain way, it's not easy to suddenly change, especially as your beliefs will attract experiences which would appear to confirm them as the truth.

To challenge these thoughts too early can be counterproductive. I'm sure if I'd left my job a few years ago I would have been a complete mess within a week and would probably have gone back to work at the first sign of a struggle. First we need to put some distance between ourselves and our beliefs. Through meditation and learning to watch my thoughts, I've been able to disentangle myself from my self-limiting beliefs and learn that they do not speak the truth about who or what I am.

Once we have learned to distance ourselves from our beliefs about who we are, we can start to challenge their validity. We can take some action that will break the cycle and finally transcend the belief we've been holding onto. Start with small steps at first; mine were doing the course and sending off the *Tiny Buddha* article, both of which gave me the confidence to believe that I *do* have the talent to make writing part of my career, which helped me to take the final leap and leave work.

After first dipping your toe in the water, the challenges can get bigger and bigger, until you see how false the beliefs are. It doesn't necessarily mean they'll disappear. I still get my inner critic coming in and telling me I'm nuts occasionally, but I've learned to just say 'Hello' and let her ramble away while I get on with my work.

Unhealthy habits

Many of us stick to habits that don't really help us because we believe it helps form our identity. Maybe you don't lose weight because you've always been 'the fat one', or you don't give up smoking because you're famous for always having a fag in your hand.

As well as cutting down on drinking, I have also recently become a recovering teaoholic. I love tea. I used to have about three cups before I got up; I have no idea how many I used to drink every day. Wherever I went I was known for my attachment to drinking tea. It was just about the only thing that gave me a personality.

When I was told by a nutritionist that I should reduce the amount of tea I drank to two cups a day, I couldn't believe my ears. Apparently the amount of sugar creeping in (one spoonful per cup) wasn't good for me and the tea itself was suppressing my appetite. Her words rang in my ears; was this woman mad? I was a chain tea-drinker! I couldn't give it up! It's what I did! I drank tea! I had to go to my mum's the following week. Whatever would she say?

Not a lot, as it happens. In reality, no one but me could have cared less what I drank. The identity was all in my head.

Again, we need to mentally distance ourselves from our habits before we attempt to change them and know that they don't represent who we really are. They're just something we do and they can change as you begin to change the way you see yourself.

Once I let go of the identity I had created for myself, I actually found it surprisingly easy to stop drinking so much tea. Since then I've been eating more (which in my case is a good thing) and have been introduced to the delights of drinking water. I'm feeling healthier, and have noticed a change for the better in my complexion and overall appearance. Silly as it may sound, letting go of my identity as the girl who only drinks tea was another step I needed to take to create a healthier lifestyle.

Belongings

I'm a strong believer that we need to de-clutter our lives in order to think clearly and make progress in our lives. However, there are times when I still hold on to items because I'm convinced I might need them one day.

A couple of months back I decided to have a sort out and get rid of anything I thought might be holding me back. So I looked through all my cupboards and in my wardrobe and found all the photos I had taken on my travels. I hardly ever looked at these photos; they reminded me of a period in my life when I was deeply unhappy. Just seeing the big bin liner which held them all made me feel depressed. I had thought about binning them several times but doing so was incredibly difficult. What if I needed them? What if someone wanted to see them? Maybe I'd have kids one day and they'd want to have a look!

Now though, I decided it was time to let go. I was being stupid; I'd barely looked at these photos in years. Suddenly, something came over me and I ruthlessly chucked them all in the bin. *There! I'd done it!* I was so proud of myself.

Then, I caught sight of my 'Sydney Climb' photo. I never looked at it myself but I had recently used it to prove to a student that I once climbed the Sydney Harbour Bridge. It was the first time I'd taken it out in eight years. Still, who knew when I might need it again?

So I fished all my photos out immediately. *I can't do it*, I decided. *I'll just have to sort through them later.* Decide which ones to keep and get rid of the rest.

Later.

It was another week until I decided to take them out of the drawer I'd put them in and sort through them again. When I did, I was faced with pictures of people I didn't remember the names of, people I didn't want to remember the names of, places I had no hope of identifying if my life depended on it and pictures of me in the pub.

I could just see me and my imaginary children now:

Kids: 'Mummy, who's that strange looking man you're drinking with?'

Me: 'Erm…'

All my photos went in the bin (even the Sydney Harbour one!) and I haven't regretted it since. It's like a big weight has been lifted from my mind; I feel so much freer, knowing those photos are no longer there to remind me of my old, unhappy self.

If you find you're surrounded by objects that you no longer

use, ask yourself why you're hanging on to them. Do you really think you'll need them at some point or does it just feel too much of an emotional wrench to let them go?

It's always going to be scary to let go of the person you've been up until now, but doing so is the only way to move forward. Sometimes it can be painful. There are times when I find myself crying at the emotional upheaval of it all. But it's not a cry of despair or distress that we might expect from letting things go. It's not a sadness that is making me cry; it feels more like a cleansing. Like I'm releasing myself from the past to discover what's waiting for me in my future; to allow the new to come in.

We fear change, even if where we are right now isn't satisfying to us, but change is inevitable. We're always changing, all the time. Nothing in life stays the same forever. We crave security, but when we get it, before long we begin to feel stifled and unfulfilled, because that's not how things are supposed to be. We're supposed to grow in order to expand and move on. We need to have the courage to break free from our comfort zone and let go of who we thought we were in order to grow into who we want to become.

Conclusion

At the beginning of this book I told you I've become a happier person. I also said that I'm not deliriously happy all the time. There are still days when I don't feel good. Personally, I find it easier to identify and relate to teachers or writers in this field who are honest about the fact they still find it a struggle. I find it hard to really believe in those who claim to have it all worked out; and if I do believe them, it then seems like some unattainable goal I've got to work towards, which just leads to frustration that I'm not 'there' yet. This is why I want to be honest with you.

It's hard to pull yourself out of negativity. It takes a lifetime to make you the way you are; it may take a lifetime to break the habits that have caused you pain up until now. Sometimes I still get down, but it's a different kind of down to the ones I used to have. In the past I would have allowed these feelings to take over. Maybe I would have tried doing something to make myself feel better; gone for a walk, got drunk, gone out for the day, but it didn't really help, the feeling was still there. Most of the time, I'd just sit on my own feeling depressed, crying about my wretched life.

When I began to understand that I was the creator of my own misery, I felt overwhelmed with how many issues I had; how would I conquer them all? Where should I start? It all seemed so complicated. Part of me just wanted to give up before I'd even started. But once you *do* start, the only way is forward.

With each move I made, with each pattern challenged or conquered, a new layer was revealed to me. I started by learning how to be more assertive, then I realised I needed to calm down and deal with my anger, which lead me to meditation and yoga.

With that, I began to feel more confident; I took up more hobbies, started eating more healthily and I started feeling better about myself. When I started yoga, I would never have imagined that just over a year later I'd have left work, would be working on my first book and taking my first steps towards self-employment.

However, the best part of this project for me is that I'm sharing my thoughts and feelings with you, in the hope that they might be of some use. After a lifetime of hiding myself, I'm putting myself out there and embracing the possibility of major rejection and ridicule. That's my achievement.

At times it will feel that you're going backwards; at times you'll hate yourself and want to give up. But try to see the setbacks as a chance to learn; as an indicator of what you've got to work on and of where you are on your 'path'.

Whereas at the beginning of this process, I'd read my self-help books and do the exercises only when I had the time, my life has now become one massive personal development book; every day, every moment is a chance to grow. I'm constantly watching my thoughts and emotions, looking for new challenges and new ways to move forward. It's still tough sometimes. I still have my down moments, but these too have become part of my practice.

Take one step today, then another, then another, then another. In all probability, you'll never be finished. There'll always be something to work on, you'll always be growing.

And that's a good thing. Don't fight whatever's happening in your life, take everything in it as a chance to learn and grow. In time you'll come to enjoy the process, even with all its ups and downs. New insights and possibilities will become open to you, and you'll realise that happiness is possible for you. And not only that, but that you're capable of much more than you ever thought possible.

References

Alidina, S, *Mindfulness for Dummies,* John Wiley & Sons Ltd, 2010.

Brown, B. Ph.D., LMSW, *Daring Greatly: How the Courage to Be Vulnerable Transforms the Way We Live, Love, Parent, and Lead,* Penguin, Kindle Edition, 2012.

Fiennes, M, *Yoga for Real Life,* Atlantic Books, 2010.

Fry, B, *What's Wrong With You: Seven Logical Steps to Understanding Emotional Illiusions,* Maraki Books, 2004.

Horton, C, *Yoga Teacher on a Pedestal: Psychological Conundrums of the Teacher-Student Relationship,* 2011. Available from: http://www.elephantjournal.com/2011/02/yoga-teacher-on-a-pedestal-psychological-conundrums-of-the-teacher-student-relationship

Kasl, C, Ph.D. *If the Buddha dated: A Handbook for Finding Love on a Spiritual Path,* Penguin Compass, 1999.

Klosko, J S, Ph.D. & J. E. Young, Ph.D., *Reinventing Your Life: The Breakthrough Program to End Negative Behavior and Feel Great Again,* Plume, 1993.

Tolle, E, *A New Earth: Awakening to your life's purpose,* Penguin, 2005.

Tolle, E, The Power of Now: A Guide to Spiritual Enlightenment, Hodder, 2005.

Williams, J, *Screw Work Let's Play: How to do what you love and get paid for it,* Pearson, 2010.

Woodward Thomas, K. *Calling in the One: 7 Weeks to Attract the Love of Your Life,* Three Rivers Press, 2004.